# GEORGE WASHINGTON

### LEADERSHIP ■ STRATEGY ■ CONFLICT

MARK LARDAS ■ ILLUSTRATED BY GRAHAM TURNER

D1450438

First published in 2011 by Osprey Publishing
Midland House, West Way, Botley, Oxford OX2 0PH, UK
44-02 23rd St, Suite 219, Long Island City, NY 11101, USA

E-mail: info@ospreypublishing.com

OSPREY PUBLISHING IS PART OF THE OSPREY GROUP

© 2011 Osprey Publishing Limited

Osprey Publishing is part of the Osprey Group

All rights reserved. Apart from any fair dealing for the purpose of private
study, research, criticism or review, as permitted under the Copyright,
Designs and Patents Act, 1988, no part of this publication may be
reproduced, stored in a retrieval system, or transmitted in any form
or by any means, electronic, electrical, chemical, mechanical, optical,
photocopying, recording or otherwise, without the prior written
permission of the copyright owner. Enquiries should be addressed
to the Publishers.

Print ISBN: 978 1 84908 448 2
PDF e-book ISBN: 978 1 84908 449 9

Editorial by Ilios Publishing Ltd, Oxford, UK
Cartography: Bounford.com
Page layout by Myriam Bell Design, France
Index by David Worthington
Originated by Blenheim Colour Ltd, Oxford
Printed in China through Worldprint Ltd
Typeset in Stone Serif and Officina Sans

11 12 13 14 15   10 9 8 7 6 5 4 3 2 1

A CIP catalog record for this book is available from the British Library.

www.ospreypublishing.com

## Dedication

This book is dedicated to my brother George.

## Acknowledgements

I would like to thank Bruce Biskup, a coworker and fellow George
Washington enthusiast, for helping me find some of the material I used to
write this book.

## Cover image

US Army.

## Artist's note

Readers may care to note that the original paintings from which the color
plates in this book were prepared are available for private sale. All
reproduction copyright whatsoever is retained by the Publishers. All
enquiries should be addressed to:

Graham Turner, PO Box 88, Chesham, Buckinghamshire, UK

The Publishers regret that they can enter into no correspondence upon
this matter.

## Author's Note:

The following abbreviations indicate the sources of the illustrations used
in this volume:

USAHI – The United States Army Heritage Institute
USA – The United States Army
LOC – Library of Congress, Washington, DC
AotC – The Architect of the Capitol (the office responsible for
maintaining the Capitol Building in Washington DC)
AC – Author's collection

Other sources are listed in full.

## The Woodland Trust

Osprey Publishing are supporting the Woodland Trust, the UK's leading
woodland conservation charity, by funding the dedication of trees.

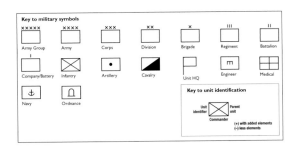

# CONTENTS

# INTRODUCTION

George Washington may be history's most underrated commander. Frederick the Great and Napoleon Bonaparte, two other great commanders, were contemporaries. Frederick's career reached its apogee when Washington was a young officer. Bonaparte entered the world stage in the decade in which Washington last commanded an army in the field. Both are frequently believed to be better commanders than Washington. Yet measured by results, Washington trumped both.

Frederick and Napoleon inherited formidable militaries, and both had extensive military training and experience prior to assuming command of armies. Washington built his army from scratch. The manpower came from a pool of men accustomed to acting independently and who resented authority. Washington lacked formal education, much less formal military training. Self-taught, he had never commanded anything larger than a regiment before assuming command of the Continental Army in 1775.

Frederick's victories added to Prussia's territory and prestige, yet cost Prussia much gold and blood. Ultimately, they failed to elevate Prussia into more than a regional power. Napoleon's meteoric accomplishments led only to his island exile and set France on a path where it devolved from the world's leading nation to a third-rate power. Washington's battlefield accomplishments – despite his handicaps in background and material – took a scattering of frontier colonies and led them to independence. Because of the way he led this army, he forged the Thirteen Colonies into a unitary nation that within a century would dominate the world.

It was not that Washington did not make mistakes. He made many – perhaps more than Frederick and Napoleon combined over their much longer careers. Washington's initial plans, characteristic of amateur

George Washington, the general. This painting shows Washington at the height of his powers, as commander-in-chief of the Continental Army. (USMHI)

# Overview of Washington's campaigns

Battle of Québec, 1775 — Québec

CANADA

MASSACHUSETTS

Montréal

Lake Champlain

Valcour Island, 1776

Ticonderoga, 1775, 1777

NEW HAMPSHIRE

Portsmouth

Lake Huron

Lake Ontario

NEW YORK

Saratoga, 1777

Siege of Boston, 1775–76

**Boston**

MASSACHUSETTS

Newport — Newport, 1778

CONNECTICUT

RHODE ISLAND

Lake Erie

Stony Point, 1779

Hudson

**New York**

White Plains, 1776

PENNSYLVANIA

Princeton, 1777

Battle of Harlem, 1776

Battle of Long Island, 1776

Monmouth Courthouse, 1778

Germantown, 1777

Trenton, 1776

NEW JERSEY

Brandywine, 1777

**Philadelphia**

Ohio

Baltimore

MARYLAND    DELAWARE

*ATLANTIC OCEAN*

VIRGINIA

Battle of the Capes, 1781

Siege of Yorktown, 1781

N

Guilford Courthouse, 1781

NORTH CAROLINA

King's Mountain, 1780

Cowpens, 1781

Camden, 1780

SOUTH CAROLINA

GEORGIA

Siege of Charleston I, 1776

Charleston

Siege of Charleston II, 1780

Savannah

Battle where Washington commanded
Other battles
Path of Washington's army, 1776
Path of Washington's army, Trenton/Princeton campaign
Path of Washington's army, 1777 Philadelphia campaign
Path of Washington's army, 1778 campaign
Path of Washington's army, Yorktown campaign

0                    200 miles
0          200km

soldiers, were overly complicated. They asked for more than his men could deliver, and required split-second timing in an age where commands carried only as far as a human voice, at speeds no faster than that of a galloping horse.

Yet Washington proved a fast learner. Boston taught him the importance of artillery. The battles for New York City taught him both the strengths and weaknesses of his army. More importantly, it also showed him the strengths and weaknesses of the opposing British forces, and provided insights on how to pit American strengths against British weaknesses. These lessons culminated in victories over British garrisons at Trenton and Princeton, victories that revived the flagging rebellion. Washington would make more mistakes – notably at the battle of the Brandywine – but he learned from these as well.

The most important lesson he learned was that his army was more critical to ultimate victory than territory. After New York, Washington realized that so long as the Continental Congress could field an army, the British had not won, and that he could lose any major city in the Thirteen Colonies as long as it remained in existence. An army capable of destroying an isolated British brigade allowed Washington to prevent the British from occupying more than three or four cities at a time.

Washington's battles took place during a transitional period of warfare. At the war's onset, wars were fought by maneuver and siege, by small professional armies. Commanders husbanded troops; they were difficult to replace. Moreover, individual soldiers were rarely trusted to act on their own initiative.

The American Revolution pointed to a new type of warfare, where individual soldiers were motivated by patriotism. Destroying the opponent's armies, not capturing cities, yielded victory. Washington's campaigns heralded this change, serving as the opening curtain for modern warfare. It foreshadowed the *levée en masse* of the French Revolutionary Wars. Washington was more than a contemporary of Frederick the Great and Napoleon – he was the bridge between their two styles of fighting.

Washington learned that for ultimate American victory, he needed troops capable of meeting and defeating British regulars on an open field. He also needed soldiers that thought of themselves as American first, not Pennsylvanians, Virginians, or New Yorkers. Washington knew that to win he had to chase the enemy out of all the Thirteen Colonies, requiring regiments unconstrained by regional limitations. He recruited soldiers for long terms of service, and organized them into national regiments. By 1778 he had an army that could successfully contend with British regulars in the open – as he demonstrated at Monmouth.

He built this army despite several crushing handicaps. Even after the French entered the war as America's allies, Washington's troops faced critical shortages of supplies and money. The Continental Congress proved unequal to raising the funds necessary to equip, feed, and pay the Continental Army. Troops had to build their own quarters, were frequently unshod, and had a commissariat unequal to the task of securing rations.

Washington won only three battles during his tenure commanding the Continental Army, including the battle of Princeton shown here. Yet he understood that the path to victory lay not in success on the battlefield, but rather by maintaining the existence of his army. (LOC)

Washington's enduring legacy lay in his ability to subordinate personal ambition and military capability to civil political objectives. Virtually uniquely among revolutionary military leaders from Oliver Cromwell to Saddam Hussein, Washington confined himself to military goals, eschewing politics when in uniform. He even quashed an attempt by his own army to make him a military dictator.

The path of military glory lured and ultimately destroyed Napoleon. Washington's ability to walk away from the battlefield, to permanently sheath his sword, and willingly relinquish the reigns of power made him truly great. Understanding Washington the general – the indispensable commander of the Continental cause – goes far in helping us to understand how he could do so.

# THE EARLY YEARS

George Washington was born on February 22, 1732. He was the first child of his father's second marriage, but his father's fifth child and his third son. Washington's father, Augustine Washington, was a minor planter who dabbled in iron manufacturing. In addition to four children by his first wife, Jane Butler, Augustine had five with Mary Ball, his second wife. Young George grew up with four siblings – his younger brother and sister and the two surviving half-brothers from his father's first marriage.

While Washington's family belonged to Virginia gentry, they were minor gentry. Colonial Virginia was a place of high social mobility, where individual ability counted more than one's birth. Washington's great grandfather had arrived with nothing, but the family's fortunes had risen through his abilities. Like his father and grandfather, Augustus Washington, Augustine used a combination of good looks – he was handsome and over 6ft tall – and intelligence to plant himself among the social elite.

He could afford to educate his first two sons, Lawrence and Augustine Jr., in England, but the family's fortunes ebbed after George Washington's birth.

Washington's childhood home. Despite the property and prestige he acquired later in life, he came from relatively humble origins (AC)

The iron mine owned by Augustine became exhausted. Then Washington's father died at the age of 49, when George was just 11.

His father's death changed life for the young George Washington. It ended his chance of receiving a formal education in England, so George was educated by tutors within his home, and his education ended at the elementary level. More importantly, Augustine's eldest son, Lawrence Washington, inherited the bulk of Augustine's estate.

Washington received Ferry Farm, the smallest of Augustine's holdings, and three nearly worthless Fredericksburg lots. This should have been enough to support George modestly once he was an adult, but his mother was named administrator of George's estate until then. George was Mary Washington's eldest son, and she expected him to support her and the rest of her family. She settled into Ferry Farm and used George's inheritance from Augustine for her own purposes. He did not regain Ferry Farm until after her death, in 1789.

Washington would probably have lived an obscure life tending a demanding mother if it were not for his older half-brother Lawrence. Lawrence became George's mentor, substituting for his lost father. George probably lived with Lawrence when he was in his early teens, and arranged for tutors for his younger sibling. Lawrence also fostered George's interest in surveying, a skilled profession that was then in great demand. George had learned the rudiments of surveying by the age of 17, becoming an expert during his teens.

Lawrence also provided other opportunities for George, as he had the connections to do so. Lawrence had served as a captain in a volunteer regiment raised in Virginia during the War of Jenkins's Ear, and saw action during the Cartagena campaign serving on Admiral Vernon's flagship. (Lawrence so admired Vernon that he renamed the family estate "Mount Vernon.") After returning to Virginia, Lawrence married into the influential Fairfax family.

Lawrence's Fairfax connection almost certainly landed George his appointment as official surveyor of Culpepper County in 1749, when he was 17. The position was well paid, and Washington used his salary to buy land in the Shenandoah Valley – land he personally surveyed. It was the first in a series of land purchases that he would make during his life. It was also the first of a number of difficult surveying expeditions Washington successfully conducted in western Virginia – which then included the Ohio River basin west of the Appalachians.

It set a pattern that Washington would follow for the rest of his life. He used family connections, influence, and his own impressive presence – he was 6ft 2in. tall, handsome, and athletic – to acquire a position in advance of those normal for someone of his age and experience. Then, through sheer ability – combined with the ability to learn quickly and work indefatigably – he would succeed in that job.

In 1752 Lawrence died of tuberculosis. His property went to his wife, with a proviso that if she died without children, the estate would revert to George. She died without issue five years after Lawrence, making George Washington a propertied planter.

That lay in the future when George traded on his Fairfax connections to launch a new career as an army officer. Lawrence had commanded the Virginia militia – a position merited through his military experience in the Caribbean. After Lawrence's death, Virginia's colonial governor, Robert Dinwiddie, divided the command into four regions. George Washington – at the age of 20 – applied for command of one of the regions.

He had no military experience or training, but he did have the backing of the Fairfax family. Besides – muscular, fit, and tall – George Washington *looked* like an officer. On the strength of those qualities, Dinwiddie gave George a major's commission, and placed him in charge of training the militia of the smallest district. The world was at peace, so the appointment was seen as a sinecure.

But times were changing. The French and British colonial empires in North America were expanding and colliding as they grew. One flashpoint was the Ohio River watershed, which both sides claimed. Dinwiddie learned that the French were building an outpost – which the French later named Fort Duquesne – at the juncture where the Monongahela and Allegany Rivers merge to form the Ohio.

Dinwiddie sent a small expedition to warn the French off, and tapped Washington for the job. The task was quasi-military. Washington *was* a major, albeit one with no military training, and – because of his work as a surveyor – he was familiar with the terrain. It seemed a natural fit.

Washington and his companions delivered a note from Dinwiddie demanding that the French withdraw from Fort Duquesne, and returned with a French reply after a series of arduous adventures. Part of Washington's mission involved recruiting Indian allies if war erupted; in this he was unsuccessful. The French reply sidestepped Dinwiddie's complaint, and Washington was attacked by Indians while returning to Virginia. This convinced the young man that the French were negotiating in bad faith and that they had attempted to assassinate him. His report to Dinwiddie caused Virginia to take arms in order to repel the French incursion.

Washington as a surveyor in the Ohio Country. He spent many of his early years exploring the American frontier. (AC)

# THE MILITARY LIFE

Governor Dinwiddie's faith in the young major was such that he made Washington second in command of the Virginia Regiment, the volunteer colonial regiment raised in anticipation of a war with France in the western wilderness. With it went a promotion to lieutenant colonel.

While it may seem surprising today to give a position of such importance to a man with as little experience as Washington, it was not unusual in the 18th century. Birth and breeding were viewed as more critical to success as an officer than training or experience. Illiterate and base-born louts were viewed as capable of being private soldiers, corporals, or sergeants. The lower orders brawled, after all. But these men needed officers to direct them. Soldiers were not supposed to think – their officers did that for them – and officers needed to be gentlemen: propertied, lettered, and invested in the social order.

Washington came from the propertied class. Although at 22 he owned little property himself, he was viewed as an up-and-comer – someone whose abilities would gain him the property he needed to maintain a gentleman's status. Further, being a gentleman gave Washington skills that an officer needed for command. He could ride, shoot, and had commanded others as he grew up – even if those he commanded were slaves or indentured servants working on his farms. His adventures as a surveyor provided him with the fieldcraft required to live whilst on campaign, as well as basic land-navigation abilities.

He had also demonstrated ability in hand-to-hand combat, and courage in the face of danger. He would not have survived his 1753 expedition to the Ohio Country had he lacked either. Furthermore, he had the feckless confidence of a young member of the gentry. He seemed so sure of himself that others followed – simply because they felt that anyone so confident must know what he was doing.

Yet Washington knew nothing about the military. He did not know how to drill troops or even the commands required. He lacked a basic grasp of logistics – the care and feeding of soldiers in the field. His total experience in military engineering and fortification consisted of having inspected the forts at Barbados during his visit there with his brother Lawrence. He was also ignorant of many of the customs of war.

Washington, shown here delivering Governor Dinwiddie's letter to the French commander of Fort Duquese, was appointed a lieutenant-colonel of the Viriginia Regiment as a result of his efforts on that expedition. He had no military experience at that time. (AC)

His superior, Joshua Fry, had no more experience. Dinwiddie named Fry colonel of the regiment because Fry taught mathematics, a skill believed critical for an officer. Also, Fry was older – and presumably less impetuous – than Washington. The brash Washington was outraged. While Washington had as little military experience as Fry at that point, Washington, with the arrogance of youth, felt that his experiences the previous year had seasoned him as an officer.

They had not – as Washington subsequently demonstrated through his actions. Fry, overweight and in his 50s, had Washington lead an advance party into the Ohio Country. Given ambiguous orders – to act defensively and not start a war, but to attack any French forces attempting to impede British settlements in the Ohio Country – Washington interpreted these instructions aggressively. He marched an inadequately trained and outnumbered force into the wilderness. Aware of his numerical inferiority, in an effort to destroy the enemy in detail Washington ambushed a small French force moving through the debated land. Unfortunately, the troops were a diplomatic party carrying a message to Dinwiddie. Washington's ambush precluded any chance of clarifying their status, and his Indian allies massacred the French. Washington's attack on an embassy created a scandal in Europe and touched off a war between England and France that grew into the Seven Years War.

Washington then built a poorly situated, badly designed, and inadequately sized fortification as a strongpoint. Naming it Fort Necessity, Washington marched his portion of the Virginia Regiment farther into the Ohio wilderness in order to confront the French. A smaller independent company of frontier soldiers, led by Captain James Mackay, joined him. Mackay was a regular British officer with significant experience of frontier fighting. His force was an independent company in the regular British establishment. Mackay's regular commission made him Washington's superior, yet Lt. Col. Washington refused to take orders from a mere captain, even though Mackay's experience meant that he knew what he was doing, while Washington did not.

The two forces thereafter "coordinated." Met by a much larger French force, the British scurried back to Fort Necessity, where the French besieged them. The fort's flaws left Washington's regiment trapped in an untenable situation, and he was forced to surrender. The articles of surrender offered generous terms – the British force was granted honors of war, and were allowed to march out of their inadequate fort under arms. But they were written in French and inadequately translated, and also included words stating that Washington's earlier ambush had occurred in a time of peace and was contrary to the laws of war. Washington lacked the military knowledge to realize the implications of these words. Relieved that the terms of surrender allowed his unit to return to the war once it returned to Virginia, Washington signed. It created a greater uproar than the earlier incident, as it conceded British guilt in having started the war. It also placed a cloud on Washington's reputation that took years to completely dissipate.

How quickly Washington developed as an officer was demonstrated at the battle of the Monongahela. The only uninjured officer following the ambush, Washington rallied surviving British soldiers and organized the withdrawal. (LOC)

Washington prospered regardless. He was promoted to colonel after Fry died, which occurred prior to Fort Necessity's surrender. Virginians considered Washington a hero who had been taken advantage of by the perfidious French. Dinwiddie realized that he had made a mistake by appointing Washington, but could not directly remove this popular figure from command, so he had the Virginia Regiment reorganized into independent companies, headed by captains. This eliminated the regiment's majors and colonels. Washington was left a choice of accepting a demotion to captain or resigning. He resigned.

The 22-year-old Virginian attached himself to General John Braddock, sent from Britain with two regular regiments to chase the French out of the Ohio Country and capture Fort Duquesne. Braddock needed someone who knew the country, and Washington did. Washington was unable to secure a regular commission of what he felt was an appropriate rank – that of major at the least – so he instead volunteered to serve as an unpaid aide on Braddock's staff. "Colonel" was only a courtesy title, based on his prior colonial rank.

The irony was that Washington had already improved. In 1754 he had been the stereotype of the incompetent colonial officer expected by British regulars, but since then he had learned important lessons about leadership and combat. After he succeeded Fry as colonel of the Virginia Regiment, Washington had asked to be placed under an experienced officer of equal rank. He realized the depth of his inexperience even before the fall of Fort Necessity.

Washington did a good job with the tasks Braddock assigned – organizing supplies and advising Braddock on the route of advance. Washington also had an opportunity to observe how an army ran, and absorbed the examples set with his usual facility for fast learning. He also made the acquaintance of several British officers, whom he would fight with and against during the American Revolution, including Henry Lee, Horatio Gates, and Thomas Gage. Washington was befriended by Gage, whom he would face during the siege of Boston.

Unfortunately, the good advice Washington offered was frequently discounted. While Washington appreciated British discipline, he was distressed by the slowness of Braddock's approach. Washington recommended that Braddock move more quickly, discarding the baggage train if necessary. He also recommended that Braddock outfit part of his army in "Indian dress" – by which was meant buckskin hunting shirts and leggings – and use these soldiers as skirmishers, fighting Indian style. Washington also advocated that other ranks be allowed greater personal initiative, as frontier fighting often required independent action. Braddock disregarded all of this advice, treating Washington as a star pupil in a school – bright enough, but filled with impractical notions that time would correct. But Braddock was impressed enough with Washington to promise to use his influence in England to secure a commission for him if he did well in the campaign.

The promise came to nothing. In July 1755, Braddock walked his army into an ambush whilst crossing the Monongahela River. In a few bloody hours Braddock was mortally wounded and every other British officer except Washington was dead or wounded. Washington organized a withdrawal, taking the remnants of the force to a defensible height, from which the survivors were extricated from the disaster. For a second time a British army was driven back, but on this occasion Washington's conduct had been above reproach.

Colonial officers were blamed for the defeat – this time unfairly. Washington had warned Braddock that by adopting wilderness-fighting tactics they could defeat the French, but that using European tactics in the forests would lead to disaster. Braddock's defeat was attributed to this advice. It had demoralized British soldiers, apparently. Worse, for Virginia, the British Army refocused its war on Canada proper, withdrawing the regular troops that remained from the colony.

With Virginia unprotected by the Crown and exposed to French and Indian attack, in late 1755 Virginia's assembly authorized the creation of a new 1,200-man regiment. It included a force of 200 rangers, who specialized in frontier warfare. Command of the regiment was offered to Virginia's most experienced officer – George Washington, the hero of Fort Necessity and the Monongahela.

Washington accepted, albeit with some reluctance. He had finally seen enough combat to realize how little experience he really had. But Washington also knew that there was no Virginian who had more experience than he did. Despite his execrable performance in the Fort Necessity campaign, he again proved a fast learner. Two campaigns had taught him much about the right way to run a regiment and how to use colonial troops to the best advantage. Over the next four years he proceeded to demonstrate how much he had learned.

Washington demanded – and was granted – the right to choose his

Washington's 1759 marriage to Martha Custis Parke provided him with an emotional anchor that would see him through his darkest hours. (LOC)

Washington advocated placing British regulars in "Indian dress" – hunting shirts and leggings – for backwoods fighting against the French. His use of Virginia Regiment troops in this manner prefigured his use of similarly garbed riflemen during the American Revolution. (LOC)

officers and full authority to train and run the regiment. He also served as his own quartermaster. By assuming responsibility for recruiting, training, lodging, and logistics, Washington was unknowingly preparing himself for his future as the commanding general of an army. Washington developed skills critical to his future success. He learned how to drill troops and how to fight with them – both in the conventional European style and the new, hit-and-run tactics of the American frontier. More importantly, he learned when each style was appropriate and how to blend the two.

He also learned how to run a regiment on a logistical shoestring. The Virginia legislature was better at authorizing food, shelter, clothing, weapons, and pay through legislation than actually delivering these items. Washington learned how to make do with broken promises, how to beg necessary transportation from local inhabitants, how to get his troops to build their own quarters, and, more importantly, how to keep an army together on a bare minimum of supplies.

His experiences as commander of the Virginia Regiment convinced him that short-term militia – men recruited "for the emergency" for periods of up to six months, and sometimes for as little as two weeks – were almost always useless on a battlefield. Time and again, he witnessed these types of militia troops failing to turn out for duty, balking at performing camp fatigue activities, and running away in panic at the first sign of trouble.

He learned to rely on long-term soldiers – regulars in function, if not in name. These men would stand and fight – whether employed in line or as frontier skirmishers. And Washington learned how to mold colonial recruits into this type of effective soldier. Anticipating modern military doctrine, Washington pushed authority down to the lowest level possible, developing soldiers that used individual initiative as opposed to the blind automatons desired by European armies. Furthermore, he began to value combat veterans.

It took time, but by 1758 – when Washington accompanied General Forbes on a new (and ultimately successful) offensive to capture Fort Duquesne – Washington's Virginia Regiment was the best body of Colonial troops Forbes had. It could drill as well as regular troops and could skirmish as well as Indians. This combination of discipline, the ability to think independently, and to skirmish effectively led Forbes to use the Virginia Regiment as his skirmishers in the campaign – to some degree of consternation on Washington's part, who wanted his men valued for their ability to fight as regulars.

More importantly, Forbes viewed Washington as his most experienced subordinate. While Washington lacked experience with units larger than a regiment, and still had gaps in his military knowledge, at 26 years old Washington had become what he had arrogantly assumed he had been when he was 22 – an experienced and competent officer.

Washington discovered that he had aptitude as an officer. He attempted to gain a regular commission in the British Army, but his hopes were disappointed. He lacked a patron among the senior officers who came from England. He was still viewed by many of them as the rash colonial, whose blundering had triggered the war with the French.

Disappointed in his ambition of gaining a regular-army commission, in poor health after five years of hard service, and engaged to be married, Washington stepped down from command of the Virginia Regiment in January 1759. His decision was viewed with dismay by his subordinates, who valued his worth as a leader.

A few days after Washington's resignation became effective, he married Martha Custis, a rich widow. The marriage had been arranged with more of a view to business than romance, but eventually blossomed into a deep relationship. Martha came with extensive land holdings that required Washington's attention. Since Washington had failed to secure an officer's commission in the British Army, he decided to focus on succeeding as a planter. Martha's property, combined with those he had inherited when Lawrence's widow had died, transformed Washington into a major landowner.

It would be 16 years before he took up the sword again, spending the intervening years as a successful planter. Yet Washington's military career remained an important influence in his life. He did not think of himself as George Washington esquire, but as Colonel George Washington.

One result was that as the Colonies slipped away from the mother country, Washington thought of himself as a soldier first. The association between Washington and military life was so strong that when he was elected as a Virginia delegate to the First Continental Congress in 1774 he attended the body in uniform.

The earliest portrait of George Washington, painted in 1772, shows him in his uniform as colonel of the Virginia Regiment. (LOC)

# THE HOUR OF DESTINY

Shortly after the First Continental Congress began meeting, the frictions between Britain and its North American colonies flared into open confrontation in Massachusetts. When British soldiers attempted to collect the contents of militia arsenals at Lexington and Concord on April 19, 1775, they were met with armed resistance. The British garrison at Boston soon found itself spontaneously besieged by 15,000 militiamen from surrounding New England colonies.

The conflict was not yet a war for American independence. Both in New England and at the Continental Congress meeting in Philadelphia, the colonists viewed their actions as a means of redressing political grievances. Colonials viewed the British army in Boston as a Tory-controlled parliamentary army. The Tories – not King George III – were the oppressing power (hence the labeling of loyalist colonials as "Tories"). Resistance would continue until the colonists' rights as Englishmen were restored to their satisfaction.

To underscore the united nature of the Thirteen Colonies, the Continental Congress – with the assent of the New England colonies – made the force outside Boston the "Continental Army," and sent forces from all of the Colonies to join the siege. They viewed what happened in Boston as an affair involving all Thirteen Colonies, not just those in New England.

But the new army needed a commander. Legend holds that the Continental Congress offered Washington command of the Continental Army because he attended the sessions in uniform. The truth is that the Continental Congress had other, more substantive reasons for selecting Washington.

The army assembled outside Boston was primarily a New England force. Giving command to a New England officer would cement the perception that it was a local army. The Continental Congress wanted to transcend regional associations and make it the army of all of the Colonies. They wanted a commander from outside New England, preferably one from Virginia, the oldest and most populous colony. They also knew that they had to give it to someone with military experience, and preferred to assign command to someone born in North America; they wanted a choice that was not a foreign mercenary.

Given those parameters, George Washington was the obvious choice. He was a genuine hero of the Seven Years War, and was a third-generation Virginian. Other possibilities, such as Washington's wartime comrades Charles Lee and Horatio Gates, had come from Britain, settling in Virginia after retiring from the British Army. Additionally, while both men had longer military careers than Washington, and had served in the regular British Army, neither had held as high a position as him. Washington had been a regimental commander for three years, even if it had been with the colonial Virginia Regiment. With John Adams of Massachusetts

While history today remembers him as a military and political leader, Washington also viewed himself as a simple farmer, and was happiest while at his plantation. He was one of the few successful Virginia planters. (LOC)

16

championing him, Washington's appointment seemed inevitable.

Washington set conditions on the appointment. He was to be the army's undisputed commander, answering only to the Continental Congress. He also made it a condition that he would accept no salary while commander, but that the Continental Congress would pay his expenses. It was a canny requirement; no one could accuse Washington of being mercenary or of accepting the position for personal gain, yet Washington was insulated from financial loss.

The Continental Congress accepted these conditions, appointing Washington supreme commander of all Continental forces on June 15, 1775. Washington then secured general's commissions, subordinate to himself, for Lee and Gates. They departed for the headquarters of Washington's new command at Cambridge, Massachusetts, on June 24, 1775.

When the Continental Congress appointed George Washington as commander-in-chief of the Continental Army, despite his limited military experience, Washington was probably better prepared for the position than any other possible choice, including men like Charles Lee and Horatio Gates. (LOC)

## The siege of Boston, 1775–76

Washington made a quick passage to Cambridge, arriving on July 2. His first challenge was getting the army to accept him. Many New Englanders resented a "foreign" officer being sent to command them, especially since the vast bulk of the army outside Boston was still made up of militiamen from New York and the New England colonies. The only contribution from other states was a few hundred riflemen from Pennsylvania, Maryland, and Virginia – and they had not yet arrived.

Patience, together with Washington's commanding presence, helped solve this problem. Washington understood the colonial soldier from his experience in the previous war. He knew that they respected men who led by example and demonstrated competence. He soon won their confidence by doing both.

Another immediate problem faced by Washington was his officer corps. The Continental Congress mixed the seniority of officers when it created the Continental Army, leaving many officers under the command of men who had formerly been their subordinates. Demoted officers felt that their honor had been impugned. Washington used his position as commander-in-chief to fix egregious misplacements. When he could not, if he felt the passed-over officer was valuable, Washington would assign the man to an independent command. Otherwise, he accepted a resignation, with appropriate words of sympathy. These were sincere; Washington had experienced the same slight.

The independent commands resulted because Washington could not immediately take Boston. The British garrison numbered only 5,000 men,

The Continental Army besieging Boston was made up of volunteers from Massachusetts and the surrounding states. They marched off with more enthusiasm than martial training or equipment. (LOC)

while the Continental Army outside Boston ranged from 16,000 to 20,000 men, but Boston was on a peninsula, and the only overland route was through the narrow and heavily fortified Boston Neck. Unable to force the Neck, the other ways that the Continentals could force the British garrison to leave would be to starve them out or attempt a risky amphibious assault on the city across the Back Bay.

Unwilling to attempt the Neck or risk an amphibious landing – and hoping that King George would resolve the colonials' grievances without the need for an assault – Washington was forced to wait, as summer turned into fall. Unwilling to do nothing, Washington detached portions of his army to broaden the rebellion. One detachment supported a successful independent effort in the Green Mountains, which had captured a Crown fortification in Ticonderoga, New York. A second, commanded by Connecticut bookseller and ship owner, Benedict Arnold, took back routes to Canada, hoping to take Québec.

The lengthening siege created another issue – logistics: keeping the army fed, sheltered, clothed, and armed. For Washington the problem was familiar; he had met similar challenges commanding the Virginia Regiment. Now he had thousands of men under his charge instead of hundreds. His Continental Army also faced a large, formidable, conventional enemy – the British Army.

The most critical shortage was that of gunpowder. Before the outbreak of hostilities, the Colonies had imported most of their gunpowder. In 1775 they lacked the manufacturing capacity to support thousands of soldiers. Washington's response was to commission a squadron of warships. Soon Washington had a "navy" of five small sloops. These began capturing British supply ships heading for Boston, which not only strengthened the Continental Army but also deprived the British of needed military stores. One of the earliest catches was a ship loaded with muskets and gunpowder.

The Colonials' problems intensified in December. King George III issued a proclamation declaring those resisting the British in America to be in a state of rebellion. The Continental Army was now fighting the King as well as Parliament. Britain was preparing to send an army in the spring to put down the rebellion. Time was no longer on the side of the besieging Continental forces.

One of Washington's subordinates, Henry Knox, approached him with a plan to bring artillery captured at Ticonderoga to Boston. A regular army would have found it impossible to do this task quickly using conventional methods. Knox, another former bookseller, planned to use New York's winter to aid his plan – he would sledge the guns. Washington approved Knox's plan.

Overcoming difficulties, Knox got the guns to Boston by early February 1776. Once he had the artillery, Washington developed an elaborate plan to take Boston. Like most of his early battle plans it was too complicated, and far too dependent upon his enemy behaving as expected. Step one was to plant a battery on the Dorchester Heights, where the guns would command Boston Harbor. This, Washington believed, would force the British to attack the Dorchester Heights fortifications, drawing most of the British garrison out of Boston.

When the British were most heavily engaged – and unable to withdraw back to Boston – Washington would launch an amphibious assault on the city, crossing the Back Bay in small boats. Simultaneously, an assault at the Boston Neck would pin the city's remaining garrison. This lightning stroke – to which Washington planned to commit over a third of his army – would take the city before the British troops attacking Dorchester Heights could react.

The plan had significant flaws. The British had interior lines and command of the sea. If the Americans failed to perfectly coordinate their attacks then the British would be able to destroy each element in detail. If the American troops landed on Boston were forced to withdraw, this would require an evacuation over the water – something beyond the capability of the raw and half-trained militia Washington had available. Once in Boston, these troops would have two choices – victory or surrender.

None of this mattered if the British failed to assault Dorchester Heights. If the battery Washington placed there was inadequately fortified, the British could clear the heights with their own artillery, rather than us an infantry assault. Yet entrenchments could not be dug in the frozen soil during a Massachusetts winter.

Washington solved this seemingly intractable problem using the two major strengths of his troops – their ability to build, and their willingness to work indefatigably in order to achieve an important goal. Washington had a set of prefabricated entrenchments, made to be carried to the Heights and installed there. His men created fascines – bundles of sticks 4ft long and 3ft thick. These would be set in "chandeliers" – heavy wooden frames – placed on the heights. Baskets of dirt would fill the interstices, and water poured over all. This would create an artillery-proof wall. Washington convinced his army to build these fortifications, and developed a plan to install the major part of the fortifications in one night, and then to place the artillery on the following nights.

Assembling the materials to be used and preparing for the attempt

Henry Knox brought artillery from Ticonderoga to Boston, a task the British thought impossible. The operation required moving heavy guns over 300 miles through the wilderness. (US Army)

# The siege of Boston

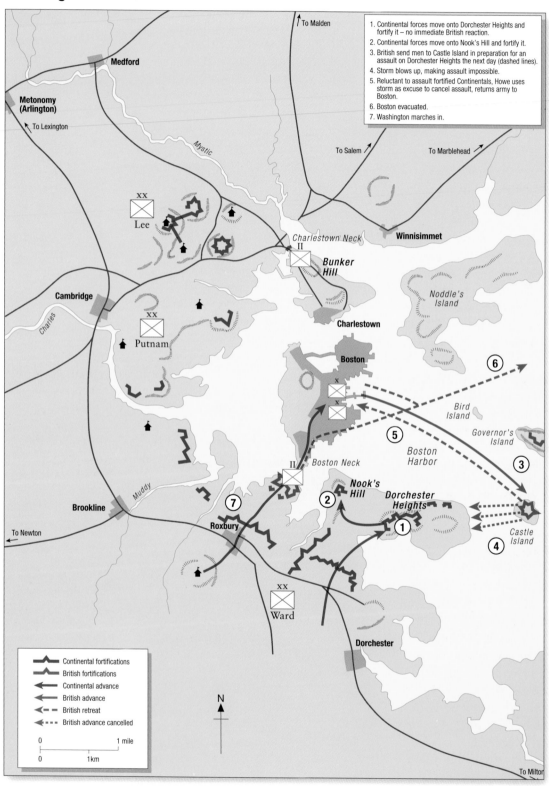

1. Continental forces move onto Dorchester Heights and fortify it – no immediate British reaction.
2. Continental forces move onto Nook's Hill and fortify it.
3. British send men to Castle Island in preparation for an assault on Dorchester Heights the next day (dashed lines).
4. Storm blows up, making assault impossible.
5. Reluctant to assault fortified Continentals, Howe uses storm as excuse to cancel assault, returns army to Boston.
6. Boston evacuated.
7. Washington marches in.

To Malden

Medford

Metonomy (Arlington)

To Lexington

Mystic

To Salem

To Marblehead

Winnisimmet

XX
Lee

Charlestown Neck

II
Bunker Hill

Noddle's Island

Cambridge

Charles

XX
Putnam

Charlestown

Boston

Bird Island

Governor's Island

6

x
x

5

3

Boston Harbor

II
Boston Neck

Nook's Hill

Dorchester Heights

Castle Island

Muddy

Brookline

2

7

1

4

To Newton

Roxbury

XX
Ward

Dorchester

To Milton

## Legend

- Continental fortifications
- British fortifications
- Continental advance
- British advance
- British retreat
- British advance cancelled

0 — 1 mile
0 — 1km

N

took two months, but Washington's plan exceeded all expectations. News of the preparations was kept from the British. His men assembled the fortifications in a single night, working silently. The first warning that the British garrison had of the new danger to Boston was at dawn on March 2, when they saw the new fortifications. Two days later, with the guns emplaced, the Continental Army began bombarding Boston from Dorchester Heights.

Although New York had the largest percentage of loyalists in the Thirteen Colonies, the initial reaction to news of the Declaration of Independence was enthusiastic. A crowd tore down this equestrian statue of King George III. The statue was melted down and used to make bullets. (LOC)

The ultimate British response surprised Washington, but delighted the Continental soldiers. Instead of attacking the American position on Dorchester Heights, British General William Howe, commanding the Boston garrison, ordered its evacuation to Halifax. While Howe made some initial moves to attack the Heights, he seized on a storm as an excuse to cancel the assault. Howe did not feel that the cost of retaking the Heights was worthwhile.

Howe knew that his position in Boston was untenable unless he did so, but the town was poorly situated for putting down a revolt. Plans were already in hand to shift the British to New York City, so rather than pay the high cost of holding the strategically sterile Boston, Howe left. By doing this, he kept Washington from launching the amphibious assault across the Back Bay that risked transforming Washington's brilliant triumph into a disastrous reverse. Instead, George Washington, although disappointed at not having defeated the British in battle, rode victoriously into Boston on March 18.

## The battle for New York City, 1776

The British departure from Boston did not end the conflict. Washington knew that the garrison would return, along with massive reinforcements from Britain itself. The logical location for a new British effort was New York City, then confined to the southern tip of Manhattan Island. It was next to a magnificent deepwater harbor, and was the Colonies' largest seaport. It could easily be defended by any nation that commanded the sea, and it had the greatest level of loyalist support of any of the Thirteen Colonies.

Although Washington felt that New York was indefensible, he was loath to simply abandon it, and began shifting regiments from Boston to New York in May. To guard the many approaches to the city, Washington divided his forces. One detachment was left in New York City, fortifying its harbor, whilst much of Washington's force was sent to Long Island, where they built a fortified encampment on the heights around Brooklyn – then a small hamlet.

Troops were also sent to Paulus Hook (on the Jersey side of the Hudson, opposite New York City), to the northern end of Manhattan Island, and on the Jersey side of the Hudson opposite that garrison. These three groups were to create fortifications to emplace artillery, with which they would block access to the Hudson. To secure communications between the forces on Long Island and Manhattan, blockships were sunk in the East River, in the hope of preventing the Royal Navy from interdicting traffic.

Washington's plans were overambitious. Hindered by a lack of manpower and supplies, the construction of the fortifications lagged. While Washington had nearly 20,000 soldiers, most were unreliable, ill-trained, short-term militia. Even the terms of his "regulars" expired at the end of 1776. Uniforms, weapons, and ammunition were short. Washington was so short of muskets that he accepted a proposal by Henry Knox – now commanding the artillery – to convert 500 unarmed infantry into artillerymen, as they could pull the drag lines of cannon without muskets.

As at Boston, Washington's plans also depended upon the British behaving as Washington expected. His defense hinged on the British attacking New York City directly. As at Boston, the British acted unexpectedly. They arrived on June 29, and instead of attacking Manhattan, they took Staten Island. The British spent the next six weeks there, organizing their forces as reinforcements arrived from Britain. By mid-August, the British had landed 32,000 soldiers.

By then, the nature of the war had again changed. King George's proclamation that the Thirteen Colonies were in a state of rebellion meant that the Crown had rejected colonial claims. Rather than meekly submit, on July 2, 1776, the Continental Congress declared independence from Britain. Washington no longer commanded a force intended to secure colonial rights as Englishmen. He instead commanded the army fighting for American independence.

On August 22, Howe landed nearly 15,000 troops on Long Island. Washington initially believed the attack to be a feint. He sent 1,500 men from Manhattan to reinforce the 4,500 Continentals there. American forces on the island, led by William Alexander (who styled himself "Lord Stirling"), attempted to stop the British Army on Long Island Heights. The badly outnumbered Continentals were pushed back with heavy losses. Some regiments stood, fought, and held the British, but others panicked and ran. Flanked by the British troops, they were soon forced back into their fortifications at Brooklyn Heights.

Washington, who had joined the forces on Long Island, realized that his army was in a trap. The Royal Navy could penetrate the river barriers and prevent the Continental Army from leaving Long Island. Before this could happen, Washington ordered an evacuation to Manhattan, which was successfully accomplished on August 29–30. Royal Navy intervention was foiled by an unseasonable fog, which concealed the retreat until even the rearguard was safely across the East River. When the fog cleared, Howe discovered that he had been bluffed, and that the Continentals were gone.

On Manhattan, Washington again divided his army. A total of 9,000 men were placed on Harlem Heights, which they fortified, and 5,000 were stationed in New York itself. Another 5,000 men made up a thin screen joining the two garrisons.

The British attacked Manhattan on September 15, landing at Kip's Bay and flanking Washington's forces. The pattern that had been set on Long Island repeated itself. Some Continental forces stood and fought, and others ran. The British captured the city late that day. The American forces in New York City narrowly avoided capture themselves, dissolving into small groups and slipping through the British cordon. The Continental Army re-formed at Harlem Heights.

The British army sent to capture New York City, shown here disembarking, was the largest military force sent to North America up to that date. (LOC)

On September 16, the British attacked the American position there, preceding the attack with the foxhunting bugle call "gone away" – indicating that the fox had run. The insult stiffened Continental resolve. They held their ground, and then counterattacked. The British were pushed back, but not routed. Washington stopped the American advance before it overreached itself, and fell back to the Heights, having won a victory that restored Continental morale.

Washington and his army hung on at the Heights for a month. On October 20, discovering that the British were attempting to flank his army's position on Manhattan, Washington ordered a retreat to the mainland. He left 1,200 men, commanded by NathanaelGreene, on Manhattan to hold Fort Washington, a fort on the Manhattan shore of the Hudson River, which along with Fort Lee on the New Jersey side of the river was intended to block the river.

The British pursued Washington's men, catching them on October 28 at White Plains, in New York's Westchester County. Washington had entrenched in a line just south of the town, but failed to fortify Chatterton's Hill anchoring his right flank. Before Washington could strengthen this position, the British forces attacked and took the hill. This forced him to retreat farther north, to North Castle Heights.

Howe swept back to Manhattan Island, where he besieged Fort Washington. Two weeks later, on November 16, Howe took the fort. The defeat was more ignominious because the British overran poorly built entrenchments. Colonial troops had developed a formidable reputation for holding entrenched positions since the battle of Bunker Hill in June 1775, when British soldiers suffered heavy casualties storming Continental fortifications on the Charleston Peninsula overlooking Boston. The rout at Fort Washington undermined that reputation, along with General Washington's prestige.

# The battles for Long Island and New York City

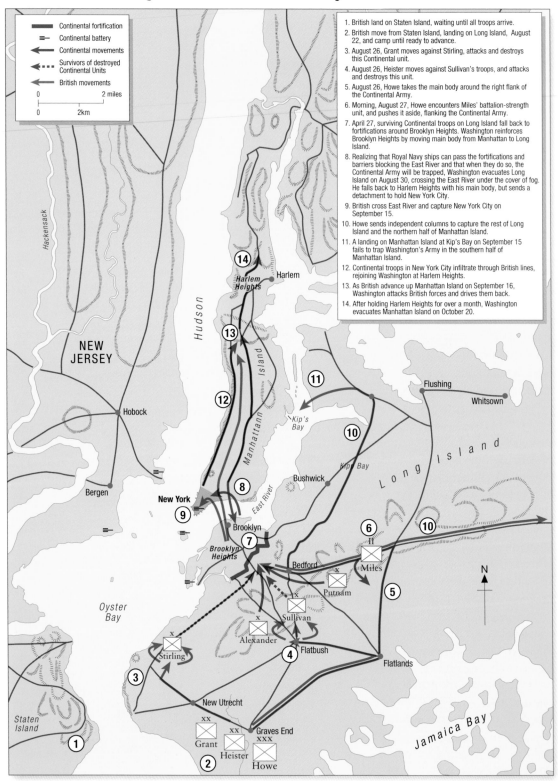

1. British land on Staten Island, waiting until all troops arrive.
2. British move from Staten Island, landing on Long Island, August 22, and camp until ready to advance.
3. August 26, Grant moves against Stirling, attacks and destroys this Continental unit.
4. August 26, Heister moves against Sullivan's troops, and attacks and destroys this unit.
5. August 26, Howe takes the main body around the right flank of the Continental Army.
6. Morning, August 27, Howe encounters Miles' battalion-strength unit, and pushes it aside, flanking the Continental Army.
7. April 27, surviving Continental troops on Long Island fall back to fortifications around Brooklyn Heights. Washington reinforces Brooklyn Heights by moving main body from Manhattan to Long Island.
8. Realizing that Royal Navy ships can pass the fortifications and barriers blocking the East River and that when they do so, the Continental Army will be trapped, Washington evacuates Long Island on August 30, crossing the East River under the cover of fog. He falls back to Harlem Heights with his main body, but sends a detachment to hold New York City.
9. British cross East River and capture New York City on September 15.
10. Howe sends independent columns to capture the rest of Long Island and the northern half of Manhattan Island.
11. A landing on Manhattan Island at Kip's Bay on September 15 fails to trap Washington's Army in the southern half of Manhattan Island.
12. Continental troops in New York City infiltrate through British lines, rejoining Washington at Harlem Heights.
13. As British advance up Manhattan Island on September 16, Washington attacks British forces and drives them back.
14. After holding Harlem Heights for over a month, Washington evacuates Manhattan Island on October 20.

24

Washington had ordered the fort evacuated, but he had deferred to Greene as the commander on the spot after Greene had insisted that Fort Washington was vital and could be held. This did not matter; it was easier to blame Washington for the army's poor performance since July than to recognize the shortcomings of the Continental Army. Fort Washington's loss amplified the belief that Washington was incompetent.

The image of Washington as incompetent was compounded when Howe's army crossed the Hudson and took Fort Lee, opposite Fort Washington. When Washington withdrew from White Plains, he divided his army. He gave Charles Lee 7,000 men with which to cover Connecticut, while Washington led a smaller force, of perhaps 3,000 men, into New Jersey, which he hoped to merge with the 5,000 troops at Fort Lee.

The troops at Fort Lee were largely short-term militia whose terms were expiring. Those from Pennsylvania were more interested in heading home than in fighting. Disease rendered many of those willing to stay unable to fight. When Howe landed at Fort Lee with a force of 7,000 men, Washington had just 2,000 effectives. Washington wisely chose not to contest the fort. A precipitous retreat followed, in which virtually nothing was saved but the troops. Tents, supplies, food, cooking equipment – except for what could be snatched up and carried – were abandoned to the British.

Washington wanted to turn and fight the British – as the Americans had at Harlem Heights and White Plains – but lacked the troops to do so. He had received only a handful of New Jersey militia as reinforcements. He also learned that the British army was swelling, recruiting loyalist colonials in New Jersey. His forces continued to fall back. He spent the month of November retreating south through New Jersey, pursued closely by the British. It was not quite a rout, but threatened to develop into one. The retreat did not stop until they reached Pennsylvania. By then it was December, and the British were preparing to go into winter quarters.

Washington had ordered Charles Lee to join him after Washington evacuated Fort Lee. That would have given Washington enough men to challenge Howe. But Lee, sensing an opportunity to supplant Washington, ignored Washington's orders to join forces. Instead, he planned to attack an isolated British outpost at White Plains. Lee hoped that a victory at White Plains (where Washington had lost) combined with another defeat of Washington's army by the British in New Jersey, would lead to Washington's replacement as commander of the Continental Army – by a victorious Charles Lee, of course. Lee's attack on White Plains never took place; the British had left to reinforce Howe before Lee could attack.

The attempt to defend New York by garrisoning Long Island was Washington's greatest strategic error during the American Revolution. The British army easily routed the green American soldiers. Only a stubborn defense by a handful of troops, such as the Delaware Regiment shown here, prevented the Continental Army's destruction. (United States Army National Guard)

# Trenton and Princeton, 1776–77

It looked as if the revolution was about to collapse. The long, dismal retreat of Washington's Continental Army sapped confidence in the Continental cause. News throughout the Colonies was equally bad. The British captured Newport, Rhode Island, in December. The invasion of Canada faltered at Québec in December 1775, but a British attempt at Charleston, South Carolina, was defeated in spring 1776. With the British pursuing, that army retreated along the route of the Champlain River back to the Colonies. In October 1776 the American naval squadron built by Benedict Arnold was crushed off Valcour Island. Only the early arrival of winter in northern New York kept the British from moving south.

Throughout the autumn, support for independence in New Jersey and southern New York withered. Loyalists flocked to the King's banners. Howe was offering amnesty, and some former supporters of independence were accepting it. Not all supporters of independence could renew their allegiance to the Crown, however. "Notorious traitors" – including Washington and many senior members of the Continental Congress – were proscribed. Howe let it be known that amnesty was a limited-time offer. Those who failed to claim it soon would share these renegades' fate.

The failings of the past five months were largely because of weaknesses in the Continental Army. Militia soldiers proved virtually worthless – unwilling to face British regulars in the open field, unreliable when in fortifications, and apt to come and go unpredictably. Militia soldiers' short tenures – in instances they signed up for as little as one month – meant that they could not be trained. Even "long-term" enlistment lasted for only a single year. From his experience with the Virginia Regiment, Washington knew that it took a year to fully train and season a soldier. By the time men had gained the necessary experience to match regulars they were on their way home.

The Continental Congress was ready to relieve Washington. Charles Lee was the obvious candidate. He had led the defense of Charleston and was a professional soldier. By December, Lee finally brought his force south to rejoin Washington. Lee felt that Washington's reputation had suffered enough damage, and wanting to be on hand when the Continental Congress relieved him. Suddenly, Lee became unavailable. On December 12 a British cavalry patrol caught Lee alone, sleeping at a New Jersey inn, and captured him. Lee's troops went north, into New York, and merged with forces commanded by Horatio Gates. Washington kept his command – there was now no one to replace him.

Many supporters of independence probably wondered whether it was even worth relieving Washington. The enlistments of most of Washington's army had expired in early December. The rest could go home – if they did not

Nathanael Greene was Washington's most capable subordinate. Yet he made a serious mistake when he tried to hold Fort Washington despite Washington's orders to evacuate. It resulted in the capture of over 2,500 Continental soldiers. It was his one serious lapse during the war. (AC)

re-enlist – after the first week of January. Most observers – even those most avidly supporting the revolution – expected the revolution to dissolve along with the army.

As Howe prepared to go into winter quarters, he scatted the British army into garrisons throughout New Jersey. It was part of his strategy to quell the rebellion. A British garrison within a day's march rallied loyalists and discouraged the formation of new rebel forces. The only way to obtain the necessary territorial coverage was for Howe to divide his army into garrisons of brigade strength, namely 1,000–2,000 men.

While Washington's crossing of the Delaware is celebrated, one thing generally not realized is that it involved the transfer of 18 artillery pieces across the frozen river. Artillery played a major role in the subsequent American victory. (LOC)

Washington saw opportunity in this. Until January 1, he still had nearly 5,000 men in his army. If he struck suddenly and without warning, this was enough to defeat one of these garrisons. Washington decided to stake everything on the outcome of one battle. He launched his attack on Christmas Day. His target was the British garrison at Trenton, then a small village. It was held by three regiments of Hessians, mercenary troops from Germany hired by the British Crown to round out their army. The garrison numbered 1,400 men.

Washington planned to hit the Hessians with a force three times that size. As usual, his plan was overly complicated, depending upon four columns to simultaneously converge on Trenton. Once again, the plan fell apart. Washington's army had to cross the frozen Delaware River to re-enter New Jersey from Pennsylvania. He only got 2,400 men and 18 artillery pieces across, well behind his intended schedule. The other columns, moving independently, failed to arrive. Washington pressed on with the forces he had. He surprised the Hessians despite the delay and destroyed the garrison, capturing nearly 900 men and killing and wounding 100. His own casualties totaled less than a dozen.

A week later, on January 3, he repeated the performance, this time at Princeton. He had 4,500 men and 35 field pieces. He asked several thousand Continentals to stay for a few more weeks, and, buoyed by the victory at Trenton, they agreed. Washington's target was two regiments of British infantry, numbering 1,200 men. The British regulars were routed. The Continentals captured nearly 300 prisoners and killed or wounded another 150. By the time the British had concentrated their forces and sent a superior force in pursuit of Washington's army, the Continentals had disappeared, carrying fresh supplies captured from the two garrisons.

These victories – considered pinprick raids by the British – changed the war. They reenergized the patriot cause. The Continental Army had showed that it could win battles. After six months of seemingly endless defeats, this heartened those favoring independence, and it convinced many waverers who were thinking of accepting a royal pardon to reconsider. It reignited enthusiasm for the Continental Army, convincing many soldiers whose

## The battles of Trenton and Princeton

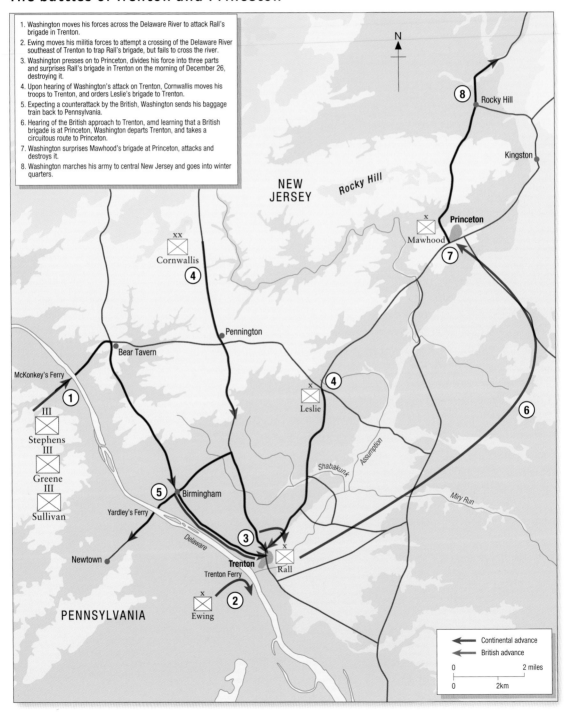

1. Washington moves his forces across the Delaware River to attack Rall's brigade in Trenton.
2. Ewing moves his militia forces to attempt a crossing of the Delaware River southeast of Trenton to trap Rall's brigade, but fails to cross the river.
3. Washington presses on to Princeton, divides his force into three parts and surprises Rall's brigade in Trenton on the morning of December 26, destroying it.
4. Upon hearing of Washington's attack on Trenton, Cornwallis moves his troops to Trenton, and orders Leslie's brigade to Trenton.
5. Expecting a counterattack by the British, Washington sends his baggage train back to Pennsylvania.
6. Hearing of the British approach to Trenton, amd learning that a British brigade is at Princeton, Washington departs Trenton, and takes a circuitous route to Princeton.
7. Washington surprises Mawhood's brigade at Princeton, attacks and destroys it.
8. Washington marches his army to central New Jersey and goes into winter quarters.

NEW JERSEY

Rocky Hill

Rocky Hill

Kingston

Princeton

Mawhood

Cornwallis

Pennington

Bear Tavern

McKonkey's Ferry

Leslie

Stephens

Greene

Sullivan

Shabakunf

Assumption

Miry Run

Yardley's Ferry

Birmingham

Delaware

Newtown

Trenton

Rall

Trenton Ferry

Ewing

PENNSYLVANIA

Continental advance
British advance

0            2 miles
0        2km

enlistments were expiring to re-enlist, and inspired thousands of others to enlist in the spring. Without Trenton and Princeton, the American Revolution would probably have ended that spring.

The battles had strategic consequences beyond their impact on the colonials. Soldiers lost by the British were virtually irreplaceable. Few colonials – even loyal colonials – would willingly enlist in regular regiments; reinforcements and replacements came from Europe. The losses suffered at Trenton and Princeton did not seriously drain the British forces, but if the Continentals continued to repeat these results, then the British Army could soon be bled white.

The American army destroyed three Hessian regiments at Trenton. The regimental standards captured there were the first taken by the Americans. The Hessians' reputation for invincibility, developed earlier in 1776, was destroyed at Trenton. (LOC)

Since the Continentals had demonstrated an ability to defeat small garrisons, the solution was to concentrate British garrisons into a size that could not be successfully ambushed, around 4,000–6,000 men. This limited the number of garrisons that the British could maintain – greatly reducing the territory that the Crown controlled. In turn, this reduced the ability of the British to suppress the revolution.

Washington now realized that his army – not any individual city or state – was the key to victory, and he now appreciated the unique strengths of his soldiers. They were far more flexible than any body of European regulars, and quickly re-formed when scattered. He also appreciated the power of artillery, as it was superiority in artillery that had helped him gain victory at Trenton and Princeton.

His experiences confirmed his belief in the necessity for long-service soldiers. He realized that he needed to build an army that could match the British in the open field, which could only come from experienced troops. He had the core of that type of army at the end of January 1777, but lost it after their enlistments expired and most went home. But as the new year began, he knew how to create that type of army and knew that he had time in which to build it.

## The Philadelphia campaign, 1777

Following the battle of Princeton, Washington established winter quarters in the central New Jersey heights, around Morristown. His march there went unmolested, as the British were too busy consolidating their garrisons. Washington's focus during the rest of winter was in dealing with those in New Jersey who had renewed allegiance to the Crown, and with rebuilding his army.

News of the American victories at Trenton and Princeton revived the patriot cause throughout the Thirteen Colonies. Reports like this one widely spread the word. (LOC)

His solution to the loyalist problem demonstrated strategic vision. Washington required those who had accepted British amnesty to appear at a military headquarters and swear allegiance to the United States. Those unwilling to pledge fidelity to the Continental cause were neither imprisoned nor exiled to the American frontier. They were instead escorted to British lines, where they were to remain until they chose to abjure the King and declare for independence. Washington prevented the confiscation of property, and even allowed their families to remain behind American lines.

Establishing this "no martyrs" policy, over the objections of both the Continental Congress and local New Jersey officials, gave Washington a significant yet bloodless victory. His actions smothered local hostility to American independence, while shabby treatment of loyalists by the British in New York City dampened enthusiasm for the Crown.

The recruiting problem remained more intractable. Few veterans from 1776 re-enlisted, and Washington found it difficult to find enough men willing to sign up for the three-year term Washington preferred. He filled the balance with one-year enlistments, but by the end of the winter he had fewer than 7,000 regulars left. He realized that he would again have to depend upon militia to fill out his forces.

If Washington could have found a way to fill regiments exclusively with officers, his manpower problems would likely have been solved. However short of private soldiers he found himself, he was flooded with Europeans willing to grace the United States with their services as officers. Few spoke English, limiting their usefulness, and Washington mistrusted the French, having fought against them earlier. He therefore limited the commissions awarded to French and German volunteers.

Washington found places for two very different French officers, however – Thomas Conway and Marie-Joseph Paul Yves Roch Gilbert du Motier, the Marquis de La Fayette. Conway, an Irishman who served in the French Army, had military skills badly needed in Washington's army – and of course he spoke English. Washington made him a brigade commander. Lafayette was an idealistic teenage French lieutenant with little military experience. Unlike most young inexperienced aristocrats – who expected a regiment as their due – Lafayette desired only the privilege of serving Washington. Washington made him an unpaid aide. Both men played significant future roles during the war.

Washington also accepted foreign engineers as officers. American weakness in building fortifications had cost Washington badly during 1776. Trained engineers, even French engineers with little English, offered a means of fixing the deficiency. Washington would soon need effective fortifications.

He knew the British would renew their offensive with the arrival of spring. The problem was in knowing exactly where they would strike. He knew that the British could come from one of four directions: they could move troops from Canada down Lake Champlain and into northern New York, Howe could march from New York City up the Hudson Valley, possibly in coordination with a thrust south from Canada, or he could go after the American capital at Philadelphia, either overland from New York City across the Jersey Plains or by sea using the Delaware River.

Washington had too few men to cover all four approaches, but by 1777 he appreciated how dependent the British Army was on its logistical tail. His main army in the Jersey Highlands could move against the British marching overland from New York to Philadelphia, or intercept a movement up the Hudson. If Howe chose either route, Washington planned to get his army behind that of the British, threatening the supply lines to New York City. Any real threat to British supply lines would certainly trigger a British response.

On the other hand, Washington's Morristown force could not guard the Lake Champlain route or the Delaware River route. Washington planned to rely on fortifications as his first line of defense in those places, as well as along the Hudson River. He did not believe fortifications could stop the British, but they would slow them down – allowing Washington to reposition his army.

A Continental rifleman (left) and a regular line infantryman (right). This is a contemporary drawing made by one of the French officers who aided the American cause. (LOC)

Howe's offensive did not begin until mid-June. He moved a massive force into New Jersey and marched south towards Philadelphia. This move was a feint, intended to draw Washington out of his Morristown fortifications and into an open battle on the Jersey plains. Instead, Washington waited at Morristown, knowing that the British would not advance into Pennsylvania from New Jersey with a large enemy force in their rear. Washington's patience was rewarded when the British advance stopped at Brunswick, New Jersey. Failing to lure Washington into attacking, and with his supply lines interdicted by New Jersey militia, Howe returned to New York, where he began loading his troops into transports.

As June faded into July, unexpected and unwelcome news reached Washington: the British had reinforced Canada. A force of 8,000 men, commanded by Howe's principal subordinate, John Burgoyne, was moving into upper New York along the Lake Champlain route. On July 6, 1777, Fort Ticonderoga, where Washington had intended to block a British advance along that route, was taken by Burgoyne without a fight. While

The surrender of Burgoyne's army at Saratoga was instrumental in gaining France's commitment to enter the war as an active ally of the United States. (AotC)

Washington disliked dividing his forces – especially after his 1776 experiences – the threat required attention. Washington dispatched four regiments from his army to reinforce American forces in upper New York, with Horatio Gates to command them. This weakened Washington's command, leaving him more dependent upon his other fortifications.

It was then that Howe moved to support Burgoyne – into the Chesapeake rather than up the Hudson Valley. Howe's goal was to destroy Washington's army. He believed that threatening Philadelphia – the rebel capital – was the best way to achieve this. Howe felt that Washington could not abandon Philadelphia without a fight. Landing south of Philadelphia, and using Chesapeake ports to supply his forces, allowed Howe to avoid long overland supply lines.

As at Ticonderoga, the fortifications guarding the seagoing approaches to Philadelphia proved more porous than Washington had hoped; the British simply moved around them. This gave Washington time to move from Morristown and interpose his army between Philadelphia and the British. But the army Washington brought to oppose the British was smaller than he desired. Pennsylvania, with a large pacifist Quaker population, yielded few militia. Additionally, Washington was traveling blind, for the first time during the war; Quaker nonparticipation meant that they would not provide intelligence to either side.

To reach Philadelphia, the British had to cross the Brandywine River. Washington believed that the British would cross the river by repeating tactics they had used several times in 1776. The British would pin the Americans with part of their force making a frontal demonstration, while the main body flanked the American position. On September 11, when the British attacked at the Brandywine, Washington hoped to turn the tables. He planned to attack the British detachment that was demonstrating on his front while it was halfway across the river, before the British main body arrived to provide support.

Washington's attempted trap failed. The British flanking force moved more quickly than anticipated, and poor reconnaissance by the Americans allowed it to remain undetected until it was on the American flank. The ambushers were ambushed. Prompt action by Washington and his subordinate commanders, and hard fighting by the Continental soldiers themselves, extricated the force from the trap that Washington had placed it in.

To outsiders, Brandywine seemed a repeat of the events at Brooklyn and White Plains. Yet the Continental regulars fought hard – even in the open – and the army fell back in good order. But drained by losses and by troops sent north, Washington's army was too weak for him to attempt another battle against Howe's united army. Washington fell back, pursued by Howe.

Washington's men moved faster than the British army. After a few weeks of vain pursuit, Howe split his army, sending part, commanded by Charles Cornwallis, to take Philadelphia. It was another effort to force Washington to fight, but Washington had learned the lessons of New York well. He was too canny to allow his army to be trapped in Philadelphia.

Howe encamped the rest of his army at Germantown in October. He did not fortify his encampment. The British victory at the Brandywine, combined with Washington's unwillingness to fight for Philadephia, probably convinced Howe that the Continental Army was defeated.

Washington sensed that Germantown offered an opportunity to repeat his victory at Trenton on a larger scale; he attacked on October 3. As at Trenton, Washington used an overly complicated battle plan that depended on simultaneous attacks by converging columns, and as at Trenton, some of the columns got lost. Two never appeared, and one arrived late. Unlike Trenton, however, the initial dawn attack stalled. It was held up by fog and determined British resistance at the Chew House, a stone building used as a barracks. This allowed the British to turn out the rest of their garrison. After a three-hour struggle, Washington withdrew. Casualties were heavy. The Americans lost nearly 10 percent of their 11,000 troops killed, wounded, or captured, and the British suffered over 500 casualties in their 9,000-man garrison.

While the attempt at ambushing the British army at Germantown was a failure, the Continental cause gained far more than it lost in the battle. That the Continental Army could mount a serious and nearly successful attack so soon after its defeat at the Brandywine convinced many in Europe of the viability of the American cause. (LOC)

## Valley Forge, 1777–78

The 1777 campaign season wound down after the battle of Germantown, as Howe withdrew the British army into fortified positions around Philadelphia. Despite British victories, the Americans had demonstrated that they could still strike hard, and had come uncomfortably close to overwhelming another British garrison. Howe was in no mood for further risks. He had taken his army around the Delaware River fortifications earlier, but if he was to hold Philadelphia he needed an open supply line. He therefore concentrated on clearing the Delaware River. It took the rest of the fall – and heavy casualties – to reduce the American positions and make the Delaware navigable.

In the north, Gates' army had not just stopped the British advance from Canada; it had captured Burgoyne and most of his army too. Brilliantly supported by Benedict Arnold, Horatio Gates had used local militia and the

The Continental Army suffered for many reasons at Valley Forge, but it did have adequate shelter for the soldiers. They lived in cabins like this one, which the soldiers built themselves. With adequate firewood they would have been warm, comfortable lodgings. (LOC)

Continental regulars sent by Washington to trap the British in a series of battles around Saratoga, New York. But like Lee the previous year, Gates ignored orders, holding the Continental regulars Washington had loaned him even after Burgoyne's surrender on October 17, purportedly in order to guard against a future threat. It was then that the British New York garrison struck north along the Hudson, starting on October 3, in an attempt to relieve pressure on Burgoyne. More like a large raid, and both too late and too far away to save Burgoyne, nevertheless it forced Washington to send his replacements to guard against that threat.

Washington wanted to attempt another ambush, but lacked the troops needed to mount another raid. Instead, he went into winter quarters in December at Valley Forge, Pennsylvania. Every nearby American-held town was filled with refugees who had fled Philadelphia, so Washington chose to avoid existing towns. He had his men build their own shelters from the abundant available timber. It was a capability that would have been beyond soldiers of most European armies, and one that allowed the Continental Army to maintain its existence without imposing hardship on local civilians.

The British held the American capital of Philadelphia and the Continental Congress was on the run; Washington's army had proved unequal to the task of stopping the British army. The American government lacked money. Yet things were not as bad as they had been the previous December. While

### Planning the 1778 campaign at Valley Forge

Washington used the Potts House as his headquarters when the Continental Army was in winter quarters at Valley Forge, Pennsylvania, in the winter of 1777–78. The first-floor dining room and living room served as offices during the day, while the second-floor rooms served as sleeping quarters. It was from these offices that Washington and his subordinates developed their plans for the 1778 campaign season. Seen here is one of these planning sessions.

Standing apart from the others is Major-General Charles Lee (1), Washington's second-in-command, newly released by the British after his capture in 1776. He did not believe that American soldiers could meet the British in the open.

Around the table are Washington and his most trusted and capable generals and staff. Seated and taking notes are Washington's aides-de-camp – Colonels Alexander Hamilton (2) and John Laurens (3). Washington's drillmaster, Major-General Friedrich "Baron" von Steuben (4), accompanied by his Italian greyhound Azor (5), stands on the opposite side of the table from George Washington (6).

Other officers examining the maps that Washington has out are Major-General William Alexander (7), Major-General "Mad" Anthony Wayne (8) (called "Mad" for his ferocity in battle, not insanity), Major-General Nathanael Greene (9) (Washington's most trusted subordinate), and Brigadier-General Henry Knox (10) (Washington's gigantic and genial artillery commander). Peering between Washington and Knox is Gilbert du Motier, the Marquis de Lafayette (11), who was Washington's military disciple, and, at only 20 years old, already a major-general.

Washington did not yet know it, the battles of Saratoga and Germantown had convinced France to ally with the United States.

While the American cause had prospered, Washington's influence waned. He realized that America's independent existence was owed to its army – his army. Washington would risk the army in battle only when he felt he could win, and only if he could assure the Continental Army's survival afterward, win or lose. With an entire continent for strategic depth, Washington was unwilling to risk its destruction to hold any physical location, even the capital.

Others thought that this reluctance to fight for territory was mistaken, especially officers with experience in the British or French armies. They believed that Washington was unnecessarily timid, and felt that their own professional experience gave them superior martial abilities. Two vocal critics were Horatio Gates, victor of Saratoga, and Thomas Conway, who had led a column at Germantown – and who had claimed credit for what success there was at that battle.

Aiding them were disaffected members of the Continental Congress War Board, including Thomas Mifflin and Richard Henry Lee. Mifflin had served with Washington before becoming a member of the Continental Congress, but had become disenchanted when Washington failed to defend Mifflin's native Pennsylvania to Mifflin's satisfaction. Mifflin quit serving as Washington's quartermaster in 1777, and joined the Continental Congress. Lee, a Virginian, felt that Washington should be doing a better job.

Friedrich von Steuben was a fraud in many ways. He claimed experience, rank, and honors that he had not won. Yet he did know drill, and developed a simplified manual that could be quickly taught to the Continental Army. (USMHI)

Washington was too popular for the board to fire, so the malcontents set out to force Washington's resignation. Washington disliked Conway; he believed him to be insubordinate and thought that he had contributed to the defeat at Germantown. The Continental Congress attempted to promote Conway, then a brigadier, to major-general. Washington blocked the promotion, believing it would place Conway over men Washington felt were better qualified. The War Board then appointed Conway as inspector general without Washington's knowledge. Washington had asked for an inspector general, viewing the role as a combination of a drill-master, muster-supervisor, and army disciplinarian with a minor function of reviewing the condition of the army. The War Board instead sent Conway to Valley Forge with the task of "overseeing" Washington's conduct, believing that this calculated insult would prompt Washington's resignation.

Instead of resigning – as Conway and the others expected – Washington refused to recognize Conway's credentials, ignoring him. Conway attempted to rally support among Washington's officers, but the officer corps proved indifferent to Conway or rallied around

Washington. The attempt to replace Washington foundered. In an age when dueling was permitted, War Board members found that they had to dodge duels with outraged supporters of Washington. Conway was wounded fighting one such duel.

The Continental Congress was unpopular among Washington's army by the winter of 1777–78. Much has been written about the hardships of Valley Forge, though the legend is sometimes exaggerated. The soldiers had adequate shelter, for example, proof against a hard winter, though they did lack food and clothing. The primary fault lay with the Continental Congress. It failed to appoint a new quartermaster general after Mifflin quit in early fall. It also failed to secure food for the army. Instead of purchasing rations, the Continental Congress directed Washington to take what he needed from local civilians, an instruction designed to punish Pennsylvanians for tepid support during the summer.

Washington initially demurred. He felt strongly that armies should not pillage civilians, especially as this alienated the population, but necessity eventually forced Washington to obey. Even then, food remained short. The British bought up most of the local surplus and the countryside contained many refugees from Philadelphia who had to eat. Washington remained unwilling to force civilians into starvation, even after accepting the necessity of confiscating food, and discovered that what surplus food remained was too meager to feed his army. In 1778 Washington finally secured money to buy food from outside Pennsylvania, but by then the winter weather and a lack of wagons made it difficult to move goods. Another problem was a shortage of clothing and shoes. By January, most common soldiers at Valley Forge were barefoot and many were clothed in blankets.

The discipline imparted through the drill that the Continental Army acquired at Valley Forge gave Washington troops that were capable of meeting the British on equal terms in the open field for the first time in the war. (LOC)

Yet morale remained high among these ragged, underfed men. By 1778 Washington's army had been pared down to those committed to the cause and their commander. Those at Valley Forge were either three-year men or soldiers willing to enlist for the duration of the war. While by European standards these men were rough, and were often viewed as rabble, by the start of 1778 those that remained were tough, determined, and innovative.

The only thing Washington felt his army lacked was the ability to meet British regulars in the open field, trading volley for volley. Washington had sought a way to provide the drill necessary for this transformation since Boston, and it was a major reason Washington had asked the Continental Congress to appoint an inspector general; Washington saw the man as a drill instructor.

In early February Washington found what he needed in a most improbable man – Friedrich "Baron" von Steuben. Steuben arrived in America from Germany, volunteering to serve as an officer without pay. Washington quickly realized that Steuben's more extravagant claims – being a baron, having served as quartermaster general for Frederick the Great, and being a lieutenant-general – were fraudulent. Washington also recognized that the self-made officer was a skilled drillmaster and a talented soldier.

Washington put Steuben in charge of drill. He created a simplified version of Prussian drill, and taught it to 120 instructors within Washington's army, who then taught it to the rest of the men. By the end of April, three months after Steuben's arrival, Washington had an army that could maneuver and fight in formation, and one that could effectively use the bayonet as a weapon, rather than as a cooking skewer.

By then, Washington had received more good news. France had declared war on Britain, entering the war as an American ally. Washington now possessed a force capable of fighting in the open field, had a powerful European ally, and was firmly in command of his army. The tide had turned.

## Philadelphia retaken and the stalemate years, 1778–81

As winter yielded to spring in 1778, Washington felt that he finally had an army capable of beating the British. He now had reliable infantry, thanks to Steuben's efforts. His artillery, led by Henry Knox, appeared ragged, but was reliable and trained. Washington had even been able to build up a competent cavalry force – light horse for scouting rather than heavy troopers intended to win battles through cavalry charges, but light horse was more suited to the American terrain.

Washington had reliable, talented officers – Henry Knox commanding his artillery, Harry Lee with the cavalry, Daniel Morgan in charge of the riflemen, and line officers like Horatio Gates, Nathanael Greene, and Anthony Wayne. One of Washington's key officers was Lafayette. In a year's campaigning he had been transformed from an inexperienced subaltern into Washington's ablest military disciple. There were still too few good senior officers for Washington's liking. When Charles Lee – captured in 1776 – was exchanged after Saratoga, Washington was delighted. Lee was given command of part of Washington's army.

French entry into the war forced changes on the British. Howe, stung by criticism for going to Philadelphia instead of aiding Burgoyne, and feeling that he had lost the confidence of the King, had asked to be relieved. In May, he was replaced by Sir Henry Clinton, who had been commanding in a subordinate role at New York.

The widening scope of the war meant that no further reinforcements could be expected from Europe. Clinton's main forces were divided, with 10,000 men at Philadelphia, 4,000 men guarding New York City, and another 2,000 in Rhode Island. All three were supplied by sea, but Philadelphia was at the head of navigation of the Delaware River, vulnerable to American interdiction. By May, Washington had nearly 12,000 men around Valley Forge, and another 4,000 scattered around Pennsylvania, New Jersey, and the lower Hudson.

# The battle of Monmouth

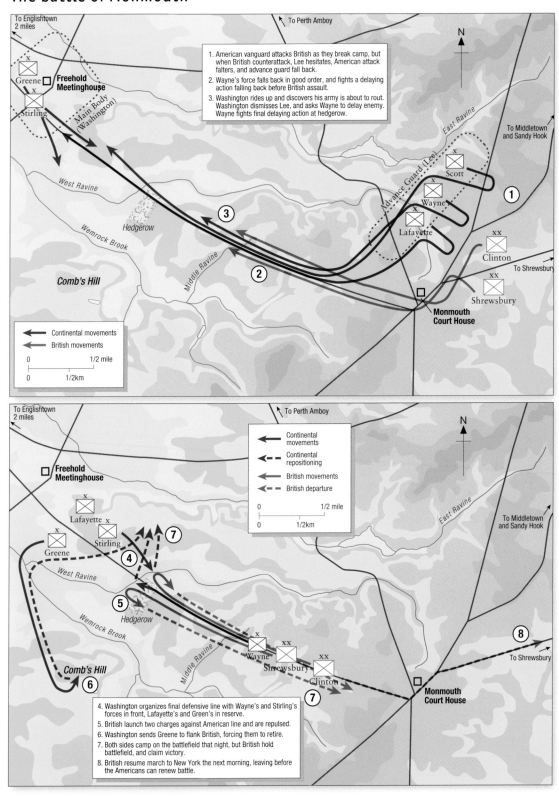

1. American vanguard attacks British as they break camp, but when British counterattack, Lee hesitates, American attack falters, and advance guard fall back.
2. Wayne's force falls back in good order, and fights a delaying action falling back before British assault.
3. Washington rides up and discovers his army is about to rout. Washington dismisses Lee, and asks Wayne to delay enemy. Wayne fights final delaying action at hedgerow.

To Englishtown 2 miles
To Perth Amboy
N
To Middletown and Sandy Hook
To Shrewsbury

Greene
Stirling
Freehold Meetinghouse
Main Body (Washington)
West Ravine
Hedgerow
Comb's Hill
Wemrock Brook
Middle Ravine
East Ravine
Advance Guard (Lee)
Scott
Wayne
Lafayette
Clinton
Shrewsbury
Monmouth Court House

Continental movements
British movements

0        1/2 mile
0      1/2km

To Englishtown 2 miles
To Perth Amboy
N
To Middletown and Sandy Hook
To Shrewsbury

Continental movements
Continental repositioning
British movements
British departure

0        1/2 mile
0      1/2km

Freehold Meetinghouse
Lafayette
Stirling
Greene
West Ravine
Hedgerow
Comb's Hill
Wemrock Brook
Middle Ravine
East Ravine
Wayne
Shrewsbury
Clinton
Monmouth Court House

4. Washington organizes final defensive line with Wayne's and Stirling's forces in front, Lafayette's and Green's in reserve.
5. British launch two charges against American line and are repulsed.
6. Washington sends Greene to flank British, forcing them to retire.
7. Both sides camp on the battlefield that night, but British hold battlefield, and claim victory.
8. British resume march to New York the next morning, leaving before the Americans can renew battle.

Charles Lee fancied himself a better general than Washington, but after his release by the British he failed to realize the qualitative difference between the Continental Army of 1776 and the Continental Army of 1778. Lee's hesitation at Monmouth created a crisis that was averted only by Washington's exertions. (LOC)

Philadelphia loyalists, however vocal in their support, were unwilling to fight for the Crown. The Philadelphia and New York garrisons could not support each other, and the New York garrison was too weak to withstand Washington's full army. Clinton decided to consolidate, abandoning Philadelphia and marching his army overland to New York on June 18, 1778.

Washington knew that he had parity with the withdrawing British, and was determined to strike at their rearguard as they retreated. If he could whittle down the retreating forces, Washington would then have a sufficient numerical superiority over the remaining British troops to defeat them in battle. Washington caught up with the British at Monmouth Courthouse in New Jersey, and attacked on June 27.

Washington had sent Charles Lee ahead the previous night, with 4,000 men. Lee's force had the task of pinning the British, to allow the rest of Washington's army – some 7,000 men – to maneuver on them. Lee, who believed that Washington's army still consisted of the untrained levies of 1776, advised against attacking British regulars in the open. His advice was rejected. As Washington's second-in-command, Lee demanded and was given command of the advance force.

Lee's morning attack was uncoordinated and half-hearted. As a result, units began to fall back. Lee interpreted this as proof that American troops were unable to fight the British in the open, and ordered a retreat. This became increasingly disordered as Lee's troops sensed his uncertainty. Washington rode up to find Lee's troops in full retreat, and the British in pursuit. Learning that the retreat had been precipitated by Lee's panic, and buoyed by the arrival of Wayne's division – retreating in good order following the collapse of the advance guard around them – Washington relieved Lee and ordered the retreat halted. While Wayne fought a delaying action, Washington organized a new defensive position, two miles behind the original American lines.

When the British attacked that line they received an unpleasant surprise. Two charges – the first by cavalry, and a bayonet charge by regular infantry – were repulsed by the Continentals, scattered by disciplined and heavy fire. The British were then flanked by a body from Washington's main force and forced to retreat. It was late afternoon by then. Both sides were exhausted, and Washington could not follow up his gains until the following day. When dawn broke on June 28 it revealed an empty British camp; they had slipped away in the night.

Monmouth was technically a British victory, but Washington and Clinton both recognized the implications of the battle. American soldiers could now match British regulars in open combat. The war had changed. Since 1775, and the battle of Bunker Hill, the British knew that attacking entrenched American troops was bloody. For three years the British had tried to force the Continental Army to fight in the open, using maneuver to force the Americans out of their entrenchments. Clinton now realized that fighting Continental regulars in the open would now be just as costly. Indeed, the exchange rate would favor the Americans. The British had fewer soldiers and those they had were harder to replace. In 1778, as a result of the war's widening scope, Clinton lost one-third of his army; they were sent to the Caribbean to meet an urgent need for troops. A lack of numbers now forced Clinton to avoid open combat with American regulars.

Two years of stalemate resulted. The British waited doggedly within their New York fortifications. Washington sought vainly for some way to successfully either storm New York or force the British into open battle. Much happened, but little contributed to a decisive victory for either side.

Jean-Baptiste Donatien de Vimeur, comte de Rochambeau, commanded the French Army sent to America to aid the United States (LOC)

For Washington it was a period of intense frustration. He believed that the United States would eventually win, but worried about the nation that would emerge as a result. Washington's nightmare was a peace that allowed Britain to keep territory the Crown controlled at hostilities' end. That would give the Britain claim to Manhattan, Staten, and Long Islands, and with them control of the mouth of the Hudson, crippling the resulting United States. All communications between New England and the rest of the country would be forced to go through British territory or make long and arduous detours to avoid the British enclave. So he camped outside New York, awaiting an opportunity to capture it.

Those years required all the patience that Washington could muster. While the quality of his individual soldiers remained high, their numbers remained small – sometimes under 5,000 regulars, and rarely over 10,000. Supplies and pay remained meager. Even after France's entry into the war, the Continental Army remained on short rations. Living conditions in winter quarters during 1778–79, and especially during 1779–80, were even more wretched than at Valley Forge. Pay was so inadequate that even officers were being forced into poverty in order to pay for their food, uniforms, and lodgings.

The reasons for these shortcomings lay in the Continental Congress. A weak body, it had no ability to compel the states, where the real power lay. The Continental Congress could issue money, but not levy taxes. Taxes to pay for the money the Continental Congress printed had to come from individual states, which were reluctant to authorize any. The Continental Congress representatives of 1776 had either returned to their states or joined the Continental Army, and those elected to the Continental Congress after 1777 were second-rate. The Continental Congress passed

PLAN of the CITY of NEW YORK

New York City was the prize sought by Washington since the city's capture in 1776 through to the war's end in 1782. Its recapture was an obsession for him from 1778 on. (LOC)

meaningless resolutions, printed unbacked money, and managed the Continental Army.

The result was runaway inflation, making it difficult to purchase supplies, pay adequate recruiting bonuses, or even to pay common soldiers' wages. These inadequacies kept the Continental Army too small to take New York. The Continental Congress's meddling demoralized or enraged officers within the Continental Army. Congressional slights were one of the motivations behind Benedict Arnold's treason at West Point in 1780.

There were occasional military actions. The British established outposts at Stony Point and Verplank's Point. The Americans retook these positions, and captured a garrison at Paulus Hook in New Jersey with surprise raids. The French fleet arrived in 1779, followed by a French army the next year. The Continental Congress twice drew up plans to invade Canada with French assistance (and Lafayette commanding), but these fell through. The British attempted to capture West Point, the American fortifications guarding the route to the upper Hudson, through treachery, but the plot was exposed a few days before it was to have been executed. However, none of these events changed the essential strategic situation.

## Climax at Monmouth

Monmouth was the result of another of Washington's attempts to replicate Trenton and Princeton. Washington's original plan was to have an advance force, led by Charles Lee, pin the British rearguard while Washington's main body maneuvered on the enemy's flank. The plan miscarried when Lee panicked and precipitated a retreat.

Before a disorderly withdrawal could degenerate into a precipitous rout, Washington intervened. He had Wayne conduct a delaying action, while Washington's main body organized a new line. The climax of the battle came when the British reached this new line, formed in the open behind a low fence. The British charged the American lines three times, but they were repulsed on each occasion.

The first and most critical charge, which is shown here, was made by Clinton's cavalry, primarily made up of the 16th (Queen's Own) Light Dragoons. The Continental line, which included Wayne's Pennsylvania infantry regiments, held their fire until the onrushing horsemen were a scant 40 paces from the infantrymen. Then, too close to miss, they fired their initial volley, shattering the charge. While Continental troops had fought doggedly from fortifications and had successfully ambushed British forces earlier in the war, Monmouth was the first time that American soldiers had held their own in the open field against British regulars in a toe-to-toe slugging match.

## The Yorktown campaign, 1781

The stalemate's end was so gradual that no one realized it was coming to a close. The first change was a British invasion of the Carolinas in 1780. After receiving reinforcements from Britain in late 1779, Clinton's New York garrison numbered nearly 20,000 men. He left 11,000 of these troops – mostly Hessians and loyalists – in New York, commanded by Hessian General Wilhelm von Knyphausen. Clinton took the rest – 8,500 British and Hessian regulars – to Charleston. London ordered this "southern strategy" on Clinton, believing that a British army in the southern colonies would lead loyalists to separate these colonies from the United States.

Washington initially disbelieved reports that the British were moving south. He thought that splitting the British army into forces that could not support each other was a mistake, as the individual parts would be vulnerable to a concentration by the American army. Washington was cheered when the British force left New York, taking with it most of its senior commanders. However, Washington's army was still too small to take advantage of the weakening of the New York garrison. He could only watch events unfold, and the Carolinas fell outside of his control.

Despite this, he sent 2,000 of his precious regulars to the Carolinas to reinforce Benjamin Lincoln, who was in command there. Washington urged Lincoln to make the preservation of his army the highest priority, and warned Lincoln against the static defense of cities. Lincoln disregarded Washington's advice. With a force one-third that of the British, Lincoln allowed his army to be trapped inside fortified Charleston. He surrendered on May 12, 1780. Its garrison – including Washington's 2,000 regulars – was captured.

The Continental Congress sent Horatio Gates south to command American forces in the Carolinas. Clinton returned to New York with half of his troops after capturing Charleston, leaving Lord Charles Cornwallis in command of troops remaining in the south. Gates, Washington's chief rival since Saratoga, proceeded to lose a battle to the badly outnumbered British at Camden, South Carolina, on August 16. The Americans lost their artillery, baggage train, and 1,000 prisoners. That disaster destroyed the American army in the south.

Washington then convinced the Continental Congress to send Nathanael Greene to rebuild Continental forces in the south. Daniel Morgan, "Light-Horse" Harry Lee, and Friedrich von Steuben accompanied Greene. It was a good team, and the situation in the south soon swung in the Americans' favor. In two battles, at King's Mountain in October 1780 and Cowpens in January 1781 (both in North Carolina), American armies routed and destroyed the British forces opposing them. However, Cornwallis still had significant forces in the south, including a field

Lafayette was Washington's most avid military disciple. When a crisis developed in Virginia in 1781, and with Nathanael Greene already tied up in the Carolinas, Washington sent Lafayette to command American forces there, a task he executed with competence. (LOC)

force of nearly 6,000 men. He was also aided by a new force of 1,600 men, sent from New York. Commanded by Benedict Arnold, who accepted a brigadier's commission in the British Army after his West Point treason fell through, this force began raiding Virginia in November 1780. American forces in the south were further dispersed in order to respond to these raids.

Reinforcing the south drained Washington's army around New York in 1780. Knyphausen raided New Jersey in June 1780. Washington's lack of troops forced him to stand on the defensive. That crisis did allow him to build up his army temporarily to nearly 10,000 men, after nearby states, spurred by this renewed British activity, finally produced long-promised but never-delivered troops. But then Clinton arrived, reinforcing New York. Washington remained outnumbered.

Yet also that summer, a French army – of between 7,000 and 10,000 French regulars – arrived in North America, landing at Newport, Rhode Island, which had been evacuated by the British the previous year. Washington wanted to combine the French army with his own and use it to take New York. Unable to convince them to move during the 1780 campaign season, Washington extracted a promise that the French would move during the next year.

Washington was desperate to find some way of concluding the war with an American victory. Conditions were worse than the previous years when he put his army into winter quarters in November 1780. Food shortages, combined with a lack of transportation, forced him to scatter his brigades from Albany to Morristown. Units mutinied due to lack of pay and poor living conditions. Others advocated marching on the Continental Congress, viewed by some soldiers as a greater enemy than the British. Washington quashed the mutinies and prevented moves against the civilian government, but he realized that the war had to be decided soon or his army might simply dissolve.

As the 1781 campaign season opened, Washington again attempted to convince the French to join the Continental Army on an attack on New York. Jean-Baptiste Donatien de Vimeur, Comte de Rochambeau, commanding the French, was reluctant to attack New York, but agreed to move his army there. Rochambeau had a campaign plan, which he presented as the French army arrived in July. He knew Admiral François-Joseph de Grasse, commanding the French Navy in the Caribbean, planned to send a fleet north during the hurricane season (August to October). This would give the French naval superiority over the Royal Navy in North American waters. But the British could maintain naval control in the waters around New York, negating the French Navy's value.

Clinton had learned of Washington's plan to attack New York. Unaware that Washington had failed to gain French support, Clinton felt that he needed reinforcements. Clinton ordered Cornwallis to halt his offensive, send 2,000 men to New York, and dig in with what remained at some port accessible to the Royal Navy. Yorktown, Virginia, was suggested. Cornwallis obeyed.

Rochambeau soon learned that Cornwallis was entrenched at Yorktown, which de Grasse could isolate from the sea. Rochambeau had de Grasse send

the fleet to Chesapeake Bay and began pressuring Washington to move against Cornwallis rather than Clinton. Rochambeau promised Washington the full support of the French Army in North America, as well as a French fleet. Washington had focused on New York for nearly three years, and initially he was reluctant, but eventually agreed. It was not what he wanted to do, but it offered the best chance in three years of destroying a major British force.

Royal Navy attempts to relieve Conwallis's force at Yorktown were checked by the French Navy in a battle off the Virginia Capes, on September 5, 1781. (US Navy Heritage and History Command)

Washington did not – as legend credits – create the strategic concept of the Yorktown campaign, but once he had committed himself no single individual was more responsible for its success. Executing the plan required the overland movement of two armies and over 7,000 men from Connecticut and New York to Virginia. It also required masking this movement from the British. Once Washington moved his army south, the Continental forces guarding New York would be scarecrow garrisons – too small for any purpose except convincing the British within New York City that Washington and his French allies were awaiting the right moment to pounce.

The army began its long march in August. Over 3,000 Continental regulars and 4,000 French troops set out from New York. The move was accomplished without the British at either New York City or Yorktown realizing that their enemy was shifting a large force against Cornwallis. The first intimation that Cornwallis had of trouble was when de Grasse's fleet arrived off the

### The Storming of Redoubt 10

Continental and French forces invested the British in Yorktown on September 26, 1781. By mid-October the allies had completed the first parallel of circumvallation and were almost finished digging the second. The British had built two earthwork redoubts across the terrain that would complete the second parallel.

To clear this obstacle, on the evening of October 14 the allies stormed the two redoubts. The French stormed Redoubt 9, and 400 Continental soldiers drawn from the light companies of the regiments in Lafayette's division stormed Redoubt 10. The two forces set off toward their targets at 8:00pm.

Depicted here is the assault on Redoubt 10 at the point when the Continental troops have taken command of the top of the redoubt's embankment and as they begin to clear the British from the parapet inside the embankment. The attack took place in darkness – the sun had set at 5:30pm, and there was no moon. The Continental attackers used cold steel and clubbed muskets in their assault; their firearms were left unloaded lest a premature shot alert the British. The resulting battle was a brutal, close-quarters, hand-to-hand action.

Trapped in Yorktown, the British under Cornwallis were subject to a formal siege by the French and Continental armies. British fortifications and Allied siege works are shown in this map. (LOC)

Delaware Capes in September and unloaded 3,000 French troops from the Caribbean.

They were soon joined by Allied forces from New York and contingents of Continental regulars that Washington had collected alongthe way. Washington ensured that both supply and transportation would be available for a swift advance, and completed this 450-mile journey by mid-September, arriving in Williamsburg on September 14. The combined Franco-American forces, including those landed by de Grasse and Lafayette's local forces, totaled nearly 20,000. They were made up of 8,000 Continental regulars, 3,200 militia, 7,800 French soldiers, and 1,000 French sailors serving ashore. Cornwallis had only 8,200 men.

Cornwallis dug in, expecting relief from New York. It never came. On September 5 the British fleet arrived off the Chesapeake to find the French Navy already there. An indecisive naval battle followed, which gave the French command of the Chesapeake. On September 29 the allies invested Yorktown in a formal siege, which lasted six weeks. On October 14, American and French forces stormed and took two redoubts in the British's outer defensive line. Five days later, as his bands played "The World Turned Upside Down," Cornwallis surrendered his army to Washington.

## Until peace

Cornwallis's surrender did not end the American Revolution, but it cost the British a quarter of their army in North America, and raised the price of a British victory higher than the Crown was willing to pay. Nevertheless, the war continued until peace was signed on September 3, 1783.

Washington's immediate impulse following Yorktown was to repeat this success at Charleston. The British had a garrison of 3,300 there, guarded by Nathanael Greene. If the Allied land forces at Yorktown marched 400 miles to Charleston, while de Grasse's fleet blockaded the place, they could add the British Charleston garrison to the bag of prisoners. However, de Grasse needed to return to the Caribbean with the 3,000 soldiers he had brought with him, and he left shortly after Cornwallis's surrender. De Grasse's departure ended the 1781 campaign season.

Washington returned to New York, and went into winter quarters at Newburgh on the Hudson Heights. The British held New York City with their largest remaining North American garrison. American independence seemed assured, but Washington's nightmare – a peace settlement that allowed Britain to keep the territory it still controlled – remained.

Washington's army remained too small to capture the city unaided or unreinforced, and he expected few reinforcements in 1782. New regular troops raised in Maryland and Virginia were going to Nathanael Greene in the Carolinas. A successful siege of Charleston required control of the sea. Recruiting in Pennsylvania, New Jersey, New York, and New England was slow after seven years of fighting.

Nor could Washington convince Rochambeau, reluctant to incur the casualties that storming New York would entail, to join an attack on the city. Even a spectacular victory at New York – however much it benefited the United States – gained France too little to justify the inevitable cost in troops. France remained an ally, but French soldiers took no further active part in Washington's war. French interests lay in the Caribbean and Europe.

Washington's challenge was keeping his army intact until the war's end. If the Continental Army went home before British forces departed, the United States would forfeit its victory. That task was complicated by the Continental Congress. Quite simply, it was broke. Giving the Continental Congress the power to tax required unanimous consent of the 13 states, and at least one state always proved unwilling to permit this attack on its sovereignty. The money the Continental Congress printed was totally worthless.

The burden created by an impotent Continental Congress fell mainly on the army. Units went without pay, sometimes for years. During the Yorktown campaign, Continental soldiers marching towards Virginia balked at going south of the Delaware River. They agreed to continue only after they had received their back pay, but the Continental Congress could only pay a fraction of the wages owed. Most of the money was provided by the French, who raided their war chest at Washington's request. The situation grew worse after the battle of Yorktown. The states assumed that the war had been won, and were even more reluctant to send money to the Continental Congress – they had their own debts to pay.

By 1782 some officers had had enough of the Continental Congress. They felt that the new nation needed a stronger central government, led by an individual, not a committee. In May, Washington received a letter from Colonel Lewis Nicola – an officer that had come from Europe to aid the revolution – urging Washington to declare himself King George I of the United States. Washington – as committed to the principle of civilian rule in 1782 as he had been when he took command of the army in 1775 – rejected the suggestion.

Matters came to a head on March 15, 1783, at Newburgh. Hamilton, Horatio Gates, and Timothy Pickering (a senior general in the Continental Army) assembled the army's officers at a meeting where they decided that the army as a whole would force Washington to take charge of the United States

Horatio Gates spent the first part of the American Revolution plotting to supplant Washington as supreme commander, and the last year trying to convince Washington to become the United States' king or military dictator. (USMHI)

Washington finally entered New York City on November 25, 1783, after the British withdrew. (LOC)

government. If Washington would not serve as king, he could serve temporarily as dictator.

When Washington arrived he asked to address the gathering before anyone else spoke. He read a prepared speech assuring his men that the Continental Congress would meet their just demands as soon as it could do so. He warned of the discord that would result if civil authority were overturned. Once he had finished, Washington saw he had failed to convince his audience. He then asked to read a letter from the Continental Congress. He was unable to read it until he had taken his spectacles out of his pocket. Most of his officers were unaware that Washington needed glasses. Washington explained, "Gentlemen, you will permit me to put on my spectacles, for I have not only gone gray, but almost blind in the service of my country." Washington's act of vulnerability did what his earlier rhetoric had failed to do. It won his officers over to him. Sensing this, Washington strode out of the hall.

His actions destroyed the conspiracy. Pickering tried to rally those present back to insurrection, but the army would not follow. Washington was patently unwilling to lead a dictatorship. The assembly instead voted on a resolution thanking Washington for his advice and voted to send another petition to the Continental Congress. It was Washington's greatest victory during the war.

His leadership kept the army focused on Britain instead of turning on its own government. The peace signed in August 1783, and finally ratified in May 1784, gave the United States all the territories claimed by the Thirteen Colonies up to the Mississippi River. New York was returned to the United States. Washington returned to the city he had fled in 1776 on November 25, 1783, after the British had evacuated. It was not the military triumph of which he had dreamed, but it was a satisfactory end to the war.

# OPPOSING COMMANDERS

Washington's principal British opponents during the course of the American Revolution were William Howe, Henry Clinton, Guy Carleton, and Charles Cornwallis. Howe, Clinton, and Carleton each served a term commanding British forces in North America during Washington's tenure as commander-in-chief, and each served as Washington's opposite number during these periods of command. They developed the strategy that Washington had to counter, and led British armies in the field.

By the start of the American Revolution all four had extensive experience in high military or civil commands, and all had distinguished themselves in combat. They were personally brave and competent battlefield leaders. In many ways they exemplified the best qualities of the British military system.

**William Howe** commanded British forces in North America between October 1775 and May 1778. Born August 10, 1729, William Howe was the third son of Emanuel Howe. William purchased a commission in the Duke of Cumberland's Dragoons in 1746, entering the British Army at the age of 17 after attending Eton. He saw service in Flanders during the War of the Austrian Succession. By the start of the Seven Years War he commanded a regiment, which saw service at the Siege of Louisbourg. Howe led the amphibious landing at Louisbourg, and commanded the light infantry at Québec in 1759, leading the assault that took the Plains of Abraham. He also participated in the Siege of Havana in 1752. By that war's end he was a major-general.

In 1758 he entered Parliament after being elected to a seat in the House of Commons. Unsympathetic to the Tory government's positions on the American colonies, Howe opposed passage of the Intolerable Acts. In 1774 he declared that he would refuse any command in North America, stating that even the entire British Army could not conquer America. It took a personal appeal by King George III, a distant cousin, for Howe to reverse his position.

Initially under Gage, Howe led the British attack at Bunker Hill in June 1775, a direct assault with heavy British casualties. Had the Americans not exhausted their ammunition, the British would likely have been repulsed. The battle impressed Howe with the tenacity with which American soldiers would fight in prepared entrenchments. Thereafter, he avoided direct assaults on prepared colonial troops in fortified positions whenever possible.

With Gage's departure in October 1775, Howe, promoted to the rank of general, took command of British forces in North America. He intended to remain in Boston until reinforcements from England arrived in the spring of 1776. When Washington emplaced fortified batteries on Dorchester Heights, Howe realized that his forces' position in the city was untenable unless they were cleared. Reluctant to make a direct assault on Dorchester Heights, using weather as an excuse to avoid attack, Howe instead evacuated to Halifax.

Howe's subsequent strategy emphasized loyalist cooperation and reconciliation. As New York had a strong loyalist base, with the arrival of reinforcements Howe took Staten Island as a base of operations, and then chased the Continental Army off Long Island and Manhattan. But he failed to destroy them, through a combination of ill-fortune and slow movement. A six-month

On December 23, 1783, Washinton went before the Continental Congress and formally resigned his commission, returning to private life. It was an act widely admired by other revolutionary leaders, but one rarely emulated. (AotC)

William Howe, Knight
Commander of the Bath,
Member of the Privy
Council, and (upon the
death of brother Richard
in 1799) Viscount Howe.
(LOC)

campaign saw him sweep Washington out of New York and New Jersey.

Howe's carrot-and-stick approach looked like it would smother the rebellion, but the battles of Trenton and Princeton forced him to reconcentrate his forces, reducing his ability to stifle opposition and rally support. Loyalist recruitment was lower than expected. He continued the strategy in 1777, attempting to duplicate his New York success in Philadelphia. However, he also duplicated the pattern set in 1776. He took territory, failed to trap Washington, and received tepid support from Pennsylvanian loyalists. Combined with the loss of Burgoyne's army at Saratoga, this convinced Howe that the war was unwinnable. He asked to be relieved in October 1777, finally departing in May 1778.

Howe has been criticized for moving to Philadelphia instead of moving towards Burgoyne. Burgoyne's army was supposed to be strong enough to act independently. A move up the Hudson made more sense as a purely military strategy, but Howe felt it would be strategically barren. Victory in America was not possible without local support for the Crown. That lay in Pennsylvania, and that was where Howe went.

**Henry Clinton** commanded British forces in North America between May 1778 and February 1782. He served under both Gage and Howe prior to that, but is chiefly remembered for his role in evacuating Philadelphia, and also for overseeing the "southern strategy," which created initial successes in the Carolinas but ended in the British disaster at Yorktown.

The only son of George Clinton, a British naval officer, Henry Clinton was born on April 16, 1730, in Newfoundland, when his father was Commodore General. Clinton grew up in New York while his father served as its Governor General. Clinton's military career started in 1748 in the New York militia, and in 1751 he purchased a commission as a captain in the Coldstream Guards. He continued to rise in rank throughout the Seven Years War, including a stint as aide-de-camp of the Duke of Brunswick.

He remained in the army and in 1772 was promoted to the rank of major-general. He was also elected to the House of Commons that year. When George III sent additional troops to Boston in 1775, Clinton, Howe, and John Burgoyne were the three major-generals sent with those troops. He participated in the battle of Bunker Hill.

In January 1776, Clinton was dispatched on an independent command with 1,500 troops accompanied by a Royal Navy squadron to occupy Charleston, South Carolina. Clinton overreached in the south. Underestimating the Continental garrison in Charleston, his attack there in June was repulsed. He rejoined Howe, and participated in the battles for New York. Clinton was the tactical commander at the battle of Brooklyn, receiving a knighthood and promotion to the rank of lieutenant-general for his performance. Clinton got on badly with Howe, and threatened to resign (a threat he repeated several times during the war).

When Howe left in May 1778, Clinton replaced Howe as commander-in-chief. The strategic situation Clinton inherited had significantly worsened. France's entry into the war led London to withdraw a quarter of the soldiers in North America. Clinton was ordered to evacuate Philadelphia. Instead of departing by sea, as ordered, Clinton marched his army overland to New York. This was done partly to lure the Continental Army into an open battle, and partly to demonstrate that the British could move wherever they wished.

Clinton got the battle he desired at Monmouth Courthouse, but discovered that the Continental Army was much changed from the force he had routed at Brooklyn. While Monmouth could be claimed as British victory, it was a draw that saw two British charges repelled by the Continentals. It was the last time Clinton faced Washington in the field. Unwilling to meet Washington's regulars in open battle, he remained fortified in New York until 1779, when new orders from London directed a "southern strategy."

Henry Clinton, Knight Commander of the Bath. (LOC)

Late that year he sailed to Charleston with most of the British Army. In March 1780 he besieged Charleston, capturing it in May. He returned to New York in the autumn, leaving Cornwallis, another man with whom he had an acrimonious relationship, in the Carolinas with 8,000 men. Clinton attempted to control Cornwallis's actions through correspondence. The attempt to run an army remotely led to more acrimony and disagreement, and provided sufficient ambiguity for Cornwallis to do as he chose. When Cornwallis reached Virginia, Clinton ordered Cornwallis to fortify a port and await reinforcements. Those orders allowed Washington to trap Cornwallis in Yorktown, which fell when Clinton's promised reinforcements failed to arrive. Clinton received the blame for the defeat at Yorktown, and was recalled in May 1782. Once in England, he engaged in a rancorous public debate with Cornwallis over who was responsible for the Yorktown debacle.

**Guy Carleton** was the final British commander in North America during the American Revolution, and the only one who left the post with his reputation intact.

Carleton was born September 3, 1724, in Strabane, Ireland, to a Protestant military family that had lived in Ireland since the 1600s. He was one of four brothers with distinguished army careers. Guy Carleton entered the British Army in 1742, purchasing a commission in the 25th Regiment of Foot. He saw service in both the War of the Austrian Succession and the Seven Years War. During the War of the Austrian Succession he was part of a force sent to relieve a Dutch fortress in Flanders. In the Seven Years War he fought at Louisbourg, Québec, and Havana in the New World, and

Belle Isle in France. He was wounded at Havana and Belle Isle. By the end of the Seven Years War he was a lieutenant colonel. In 1766 Carleton was made Lieutenant Governor and acting administrator of Québec. He had no previous experience administering a political office, and the appointment was thought to have been made through the influence of Charles Lennox, 3rd Duke of Richmond, who served as a patron during Carleton's career. Carleton proved to be a gifted administrator, and was successful at improving relations between the French Canadians and their new British masters. His efforts were a key reason for the passage of the Québec Act of 1774, which granted free practice of the Catholic faith and permitted use of French civil law. While the act infuriated American colonists, it ensured the loyalty of French Canadians to the British Crown during The Revolutionary War.

Guy Carleton, the First Baron Dorchester, Knight Commander of the Bath. (LOC)

In 1775 Carleton was appointed Governor General of Québec, taking command of a province that then contained most of what today are the Canadian provinces of Ontario and Québec. As the man responsible for Canada, he began preparing its defenses after the fall of Ticonderoga in 1775. He directed British forces holding Québec during the American invasion in November and December of that year, defeating an attempt to storm the city during a nighttime snowstorm on New Year's Eve.

He also led the British counterattack in the spring and summer of 1776 that cleared American forces from Québec. That campaign culminated in the battle of Lake Champlain, where a British flotilla Carleton had constructed on that lake decisively defeated an American fleet led by Benedict Arnold. By building his fleet, Arnold delayed Carleton's advance until late fall, too late for Carleton to retake Ticonderoga.

The uniform of a Hessian soldier from the Lossberg Regiment, which fought at Trenton. (USMHI)

Despite Carleton's success, disagreements with Howe and with Burgoyne – sent to Canada with reinforcements in 1776 – led to Carleton's recall in 1777. He remained in Canada through 1778, but with no military responsibility, which was transferred to Burgoyne. Burgoyne then lost his army at Saratoga, undermining his contention that Carleton had been too cautious the previous year when Carleton failed to advance into New York.

Carleton returned to North America in February 1782, to replace Henry Clinton as commander-in-chief of British forces in North America. He arrived in New York in May 1782, and conducted an active defense of New York for the next 16 months. His intention was less to defeat Washington than to keep Washington's army off balance and unable to attack New York City.

In August 1783 London informed Carleton that Britain would grant the United States independence, and that New York was to be handed back to the United States. Carleton organized the evacuation of the city, including the withdrawal of loyalist civilians and runaway slaves, and oversaw the suspension of hostilities. He completed the evacuation on November 28 and returned to England.

**Charles Cornwallis** served as a subordinate general to Howe and Clinton, and commanded the British expeditionary force in the southern colonies after Clinton's departure to New York in 1780.

Cornwallis was born on December 31, 1738, in London. He was the eldest son of Charles Cornwallis, the Fifth Baron Cornwallis. He was extremely well connected. Charles Townshend (author of the Townshend Acts) was his grandfather, Sir Robert Walpole was a granduncle, and Frederick Cornwallis, Archbishop of Canterbury, was his uncle.

Educated at Eton and Cambridge, Cornwallis entered the British Army in 1756, purchasing an ensign's commission in the Grenadier Guards. He took his career as an officer seriously, studying at the military academy in Turin. During the Seven Years War he fought as a junior officer at Minden, and as a lieutenant-colonel he led a regiment at the battles of Villinghausen, Wilhelmsthal, and Lutterberg, and the siege of Cassel.

He was elected to the House of Commons in 1760. After the death of his father, he was elevated to the peerage, inheriting the title Earl Cornwallis. Part of the pro-American Whig faction in the House of Lords, he voted against the Stamp Act. He became colonel of the 33rd Regiment of Foot in 1766, being made constable of the Tower of London in 1770, and promoted to the rank of major-general in 1775.

Despite his sympathies for the American Colonists, when the American Revolution began Cornwallis agreed to serve in North America, fighting to put down the rebellion. Promoted to the rank of lieutenant-general, he arrived in 1776 and fought at Charleston that year. He also served in the subsequent campaign in New York and New Jersey, often commanding the advance elements of the British Army. When Washington attacked Princeton and Trenton, Howe had Cornwallis take charge of British troops in New Jersey. Cornwallis reconsolidated the scattered British garrisons, and marched against Washington at Trenton. Arriving, he found that the Americans had retired to fortified winter quarters around Morristown. In the 1777 Philadelphia Campaign, Cornwallis led the flanking division at Brandywine that almost succeeded in trapping the Continental Army.

Charles Cornwallis, Viscount Brome, the Earl Cornwallis, and (ultimately) First Marquess Cornwallis, Knight of the Garter, was best known in America for surrendering the British army at Yorktown. (AotC)

When Clinton took command of British forces, Cornwallis became Clinton's primary subordinate. The two had a rocky relationship. Cornwallis felt that Clinton's strategic plans were too conservative. Clinton, critical of Cornwallis's pursuit of Washington in 1776, mistrusted him. Cornwallis submitted his resignation, but Clinton rejected it. Cornwallis commanded part of the British force at Monmouth in 1778, leading the initial counterattack that caused Charles Lee's panicked retreat.

He departed for Britain shortly afterwards, remaining there the rest of 1778 and part of 1779 caring for his dying wife. He returned to North America in July 1779 to play an active role in the new "southern strategy" ordered by London.

Cornwallis participated in Clinton's siege and capture of Charleston in 1780, but after Clinton's departure he took command of British forces in the Carolinas, some 8,000 troops. The distance from New York, combined with Cornwallis's influence in London, allowed him to operate his force almost completely independently of Clinton. This allowed Cornwallis to run an over-ambitious campaign to raise the southern colonies for the Crown using loyalists to reinforce and supply his army.

While initially successful, there was less loyalist support in the Carolinas than Cornwallis anticipated. Cornwallis moved north to Virginia to rally support there. Again, he was initially successful militarily, but failed to gain much support for the Crown. While Cornwallis was in Virginia chasing Lafayette's smaller army, Clinton, irritated at having his directions to Cornwallis ignored, sent direct orders to Cornwallis to fortify that army in a Virginia port. Balked, Cornwallis did as ordered, digging in at Yorktown. He also passively obeyed orders, ignoring the Franco-American build-up around the peninsula until it was too late to break out. Cornwallis was forced to surrender his garrison when the Royal Navy failed to relieve Yorktown.

The Revolutionary War ended after the United States and Great Britain signed a separate peace on September 3, 1783. While war continued between the European powers, Washington's goal of an independent United States was finally achieved. (LOC)

# INSIDE THE MIND

Washington's greatness was not a measure of the battles he won or his tactical genius. Many generals won more battles, often against greater odds. Rather, Washington was a great general because he knew when a battle was worth fighting and when it was not. He always subordinated the battlefield to a larger civic purpose.

More importantly, not once during his tenure as commander-in-chief of the Continental Army did Washington fight a battle to gain personal glory. It was not because Washington did not hunger for it; he bitterly regretted taking Boston and New York City because the British evacuated rather than because his army drove the enemy out at bayonet point. He wanted an opportunity to show what Colonial soldiers – the men he had trained – could do.

Similarly, every battle fought by the Continental Army was fought because Washington felt it was a military necessary. At Brooklyn, Harlem Heights, White Plains, and the Brandywine he stood and fought because it was necessary to delay the enemy. At Trenton, Princeton, Germantown, and Monmouth he attacked because a victory was required to preserve the revolution. In the Yorktown campaign he subordinated his own desires to support a plan that others had created, and which – at the time – he felt would yield credit to others, rather than him.

Finally, throughout the war – even when inconvenient or personally embarrassing – Washington deferred to the civilian leadership of the Continental Congress. It was not that Washington felt their judgment superior to his, in fact rather the opposite. Washington viewed the Continental Congress as feckless, self-serving, and venal. Yet the Continental Congress reflected the people's will – the cause for which Washington fought. He thought that unless the civil authorities had pre-eminence over the military the revolution would lose legitimacy.

George Washington's family – especially his wife Martha (far left) – was very important to him. To Washington's right is Nelly Custis, Washington's stepdaughter. To his left is George Washington Parke Custis, Washington's stepgrandson (and adopted son). (LOC)

Washington's behavior speaks of tremendous self-discipline, a self-discipline that he lacked in his youth, but which he had developed by 1775. It was a function of several things – his experiences commanding the Virginia Regiment during the later portions of the Seven Years War, his responsibilities as a plantation owner, and perhaps most importantly his marriage to Martha Custis.

The hard knocks Washington received between 1753 and 1755 did much to smooth off his rough edges. It showed him that that he was fallible, something that many prodigies learn far too late. It also taught him that knowing what he was doing was more important than appearing to do so. He was no longer the callow youth that in 1754 wrote, "I heard the bullets whistle, and, believe me, there is something charming in the sound." By the end of the Seven Years War Washington knew that there was nothing charming about war.

Washington's 16 years spent as a planter prior to assuming command of the Continental Army also shaped his perceptions and gave him an identity. In 1754 he was a rootless youth who sought advancement through preference. By 1775 he was a successful planter. Securing preference required subservience, and a willingness to shape one's views to match that of a patron. Succeeding as a planter required competence, determination, and independence.

Washington was temperamentally unsuited to subservience. Had he succeeded in gaining the regular commission in the British Army he had desired – an organization in which influence counted as much as competence – Washington would likely have died an obscure and frustrated major or lieutenant-colonel.

As a planter, success was determined by his own actions and decisions. Few Virginia planters were economically successful. Most, like Thomas Jefferson, died deeply in debt. Washington's success was owing to his willingness to make unpopular decisions and maintain a rigid discipline in maintaining his course. Growing wheat rather than tobacco was unfashionable in Tidewater Virginia, a society that lived by fashion. So was selling to local markets instead of shipping goods to England. Washington did both.

By the start of the American Revolution, Washington was disengaging his personal finances from dependence on London markets and shops. It was not an ideologically political choice. Economics rather than sentiment led him down this path. His actions had molded him into a man who could determine a strategy and follow that course, ignoring popularity or even his own immediate desires and whims.

Yet while this might have given the strength he needed as a commander, another influence kept Washington from developing into a rigid ideologue like Robespierre or Marat – his marriage to Martha Custis. Those unsympathetic to Washington depict his marriage as being made primarily for financial reasons. She was a rich widow, and marrying her was an easy way for an ambitious man to gain a fortune. This view oversimplifies Washington's marriage in two deceptive ways.

Martha's property remained her own. Additionally, two-thirds of the property that Martha brought to the marriage was actually owned by her children. She had use of it during her lifetime, but after her death it reverted to them. While George Washington gained financially by marriage to Martha, he also gained tremendous responsibilities along with her property. Washington was scrupulous about his management of this land, especially Martha's "dower" share – the property she directly inherited. Washington could manage it, but not dispose of it, and management decisions had to be approved by Martha.

Moreover, the marriage developed into a deep and loving relationship. Martha kept Washington human. She was his most intimate confidante, the one person to whom he could speak clearly. He hated his absences from her. During the Revolutionary War, Martha accompanied Washington whenever possible, staying with him while the army was in winter quarters. Her presence helped lift the burdens of command.

These influences – his farm and his family – were a major reason that Washington, unlike most of history's revolutionary leaders, did not define his identity by his battlefield successes. Washington was content with his life prior to the revolution. He was happiest when he was a successful farmer surrounded by a loving family, and he did not believe that becoming King George I of the United States would improve that.

Yet – as indicated by his scrupulous management of his wife and stepchildren's property – he was a man who took his

Mount Vernon – shown here as it appeared in 1800 – was a major focus of George Washington's life. He was never happier than when he was being "Farmer George." (LOC)

responsibilities seriously. He accepted command of the Continental Army – and later agreed to become President of the United States – not out of ambition, but because the job needed doing, and because he believed himself the man best qualified for the position.

# WHEN WAR IS DONE

After the Revolutionary War, Washington did what few other victorious revolutionary commanders did – he retired from public life and went home. Washington's ride from New York to Virginia was a triumphal procession. He stopped at Annapolis, Maryland, where the Continental Congress was then sitting. There, on December 23, 1783, he formally resigned his commission, delivering a written statement that returned him to private life.

Washington was determined to demonstrate that he had accepted the position of commander of the Continental Army out of patriotism, not self-interest. Avoiding all public offices demonstrated that he would not seek any advantage from the public purse. He even resigned as a vestryman at his church – at that time, the church council had temporal powers.

He spent three years in retirement, doing what he had longed to do during the long war years – playing the country squire. He concentrated on improving the productivity of his farm holdings now that he could personally attend to agricultural issues. He also indulged his interests in science and technology. He helped found a company to build a canal connecting the Potomac to the Ohio, helped underwrite an effort to build a steam-powered boat, and invested in the James River Company – another canal-building effort.

The war had made Washington an international celebrity. A stream of people from both Europe and the United States visited him at Mount Vernon; many stayed overnight. Others wrote, asking Washington's advice or seeking favors. Artists and sculptors came to immortalize him in paint, marble, and bronze.

Washington traveled extensively during this period. He made an expedition to the western frontier in 1784, touring his holding in Virginia's Ohio Country, and occasionally conducting a survey. Yet his travels focused on America's west. Washington ignored all invitations to visit Europe. He would have been lionized in France or Spain, but he demurred, using his inability to speak French or Spanish as an excuse. He preferred the New World to the Old World. The only thing that could have dragged Washington back onto the public stage was a threat to the country he helped found. By 1787 that moment had arrived.

Washington's Mount Vernon estate became the destination for numerous travelers from both the United States and Europe who wanted to see the former commander of the Continental Army. One of these post-war visitors was Lafayette. (LOC)

The states that formed the United States operated under the Articles of Confederation, rules drafted during the Second Congressional Congress in 1777 and finally ratified by all 13 states in 1781. The articles had resulted in a central government that was so weak that it almost destroyed the United States during the revolution. Only Washington's commitment to civilian rule prevented the nation from dissolving into civil war. Washington had hoped that peace would draw the states together into a single nation, but by 1785 it had become apparent that the nation was fracturing. This led to the Annapolis Convention in 1785 to address the weaknesses of the Articles. Only five states attended, but that convention called for a new convention to revise the federal constitution.

The result was a constitutional convention to be held in Philadelphia in 1787. It was feared that that convention would fare as poorly as the Annapolis Convention unless Washington lent his prestige to it. Washington – who wholeheartedly subscribed to the concept that the United States was one nation, not 13 – reluctantly agreed to participate. Even more reluctantly, he agreed to preside over the Grand Convention at Philadelphia. Over a five-month period – from May to September 1787 – with Washington guiding the assembly, the convention wrote the Constitution of the United States of America, the document that remains the supreme law of the United States today.

Between September 1787 and June 1788 ten states had ratified the constitution drafted at the Philadelphia convention, enough for the Congress of the Confederation to create a committee to put the new government into operation. Washington lent his name to the ratification efforts. An 11th state ratified the constitution in July, and in November the states elected a slate of electors – a body now known as the Electoral College – to pick a President of the United States for its first four-year term. The man chosen, unanimously, was George Washington.

Having created the Constitution, Washington could not walk away from the responsibility he was given. Once again, and again reluctantly, he re-entered public life. He served as President of the United States for two terms. In his first term, he established traditions that are observed to the present day. While commanding the Continental Army, Washington had insisted upon the title "Your Excellency." As President, Washington was equally insistent upon a proper title. While some wanted terms even more exalted than "Your Excellency," Washington, sensing the need to keep the President as a first among equals rather than a superior being, chose the simple appellation, "Mr President." He also established the cabinet system that is still used by the executive branch of government.

It took the Constitutional Convention to force Washington's return to public life. (LOC)

Washington intended to retire after one term, but agreed to serve for a second. His second term was more tumultuous than his first. The most important international event was the Jay Treaty, which settled issues between Britain and the United States that had festered since the end of the Revolution. Washington was able to get the treaty ratified, despite strong domestic opposition. The treaty resulted in both the evacuation of western forts by the British and the creation of political parties in the United States.

The Whiskey Rebellion – an insurrection by Western farmers against a whiskey excise – also flared into violence in 1794. Washington personally led the federal army raised to suppress the rebellion, taking the president's title of "commander-in-chief" literally. It would be the only time a US president led an army in the field. The rebellion quickly collapsed, with more pardons than fighting.

Pressed to serve a third term in 1796, Washington refused. This created a precedent for the peaceful transition of power and established a tradition of no more than two terms being served by any president. He retired for a third and final time in 1797, and devoted his time to farming. Washington died at Mount Vernon on December 14, 1799, following a throat infection. His final words were "'Tis well." It was a good summation of his life and accomplishments.

George Washington as President. While Washington loved uniforms and demanded the title "His Excellency" while commander-in-chief of the Continental Army, in order to stress the civilian nature of the presidency he always appeared in a civilian suit (when he was not leading the Army), and was addressed as "Mr President." (LOC)

# A LIFE IN WORDS

"First in war, first in peace, and first in the hearts of his countrymen, he was second to none in humble and enduring scenes of private life." So began the eulogy to Washington delivered by Henry "Light-Horse Harry" Lee. Lee was both a wartime comrade and subordinate of Washington during the revolution. While effusive by modern standards, Lee's eulogy reflected contemporary opinion of Washington.

Other men of the era seconded Lee's sentiments. Thomas Jefferson stated, "Washington errs as other men do, but errs with integrity … his name will triumph over time and will in future ages assure its just station among the most celebrated worthies of the world." In a letter to Walter Jones written in 1814, Thomas Jefferson gave his judgment on Washington's military ability, speaking of "the advantage he [Washington] derived from councils of war, where, hearing all suggestions, he selected whatever was best; and certainly no General ever planned his battles more judiciously." Jefferson also wrote: "Perhaps the strongest feature in his character was prudence, never acting until every circumstance, every consideration, was maturely weighed; refraining if he saw a doubt, but, when once decided, going through with his purpose, whatever obstacles opposed."

A mural of Washington ascending to heaven graces the dome of the rotunda in the Capitol Building in Washington, DC. It is an indication of the esteem in which he was held in 19th-century America. (AotC)

The Marquis de Chastellux wrote, "A hero in a republic, he excites another sort of respect which seems to spring from the sole idea that the safety of each individual is attached to his person." De Chastellux worked closely with Washington during the war, being the most senior French officer that spoke English.

Washington was also admired on the world stage, especially by Napoleon. Before departing for Egypt, Napoleon said of Washington, then still living, "The measure of his fame is full. Posterity will talk of him with reverence as the founder of a great empire, when my name shall be lost in the vortex of Revolutions!" It reveals something about Napoleon that he was more fascinated with Washington's fame than Washington's accomplishments. When Washington died, Napoleon, then head of France's revolution-based government – a position attained through coup rather than election – declared ten days of mourning in France, stating, "Washington has died. This great man fought against tyranny; and consolidated the freedom of his fatherland; his memory will be always precious to … all the free men who … fight for equality and freedom."

Unlike many famous men, Washington never wrote memoirs. He was a confirmed diarist, however. He kept a diary from 1760 on, although he was spotty with his entries until 1768. Unfortunately, during the period of most interest to this book – while he was commander-in-chief of the Continental Army – he was too busy commanding an army to maintain his habit. Exceptions exist for a brief period in 1780, when he kept a weather diary, and a second period during the Yorktown campaign, when he recorded his thoughts about the campaign. He did not resume his diary writing until after his resignation and return to private life. His personal correspondence, except for two letters, was burned after his death by Martha Washington.

Despite Washington's celebrity, not all of his papers survived. They were personal property, bequeathed to a nephew at his death. His heirs handled the papers with a degree of casualness that resulted in damage or loss. However, in 1834 Congress authorized the purchase of the surviving documents. Today, they are in the Library of Congress, in the Washington Collection. Along with materials from Washington's days as a surveyor, these documents have been digitized and are available online. Readers can access them at http://memory.loc.gov/ammem/gwhtml/gwhome.html.

As the young republic grew, so did Washington's reputation. Even before his death the nation's capital was named after him, as were numerous other cities and counties. His legend grew along with his reputation – as illustrated in the biographies written about Washington. Some were historically sound, starting with a five-volume biography written in 1804 by John Marshall, Chief Justice of the United States. Many other biographers were more interested in producing an entertaining story, however, and chose to portray Washington as a larger-than-life character. This school of writing was typified by Mason Lock Weems, who wrote a literally fabulous work, published in 1800. It made Washington a super-human paragon, lacking human weaknesses or vices (except perhaps his perfection) and possessing virtues so numberless that a schoolboy could absorb them simply by reading of them.

This led to a third flavor of Washington biography – the debunking work, presenting Washington as scoundrel. It is easy to do: simply stitch together all of the numerous and serious mistakes Washington made during his career. Washington's strength was in his ability to survive mistakes and learn from them, but those actions can also be attributed to self-serving motives. The debunking biography first appeared in the 1920s, after World War I challenged the "Great Man" theory of history. It has swelled since then, generally in support of some political or social fad.

There are few other Americans about whom so much has been written. One of the comments I heard most frequently while writing this book was "What more can you write about Washington?" Yet as long as the United States exists, more will be written about him and Washington will be re-examined and reinterpreted through the lens of contemporary opinion.

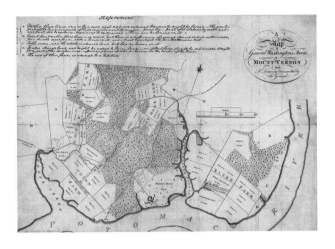

A map of Mount Vernon drafted by Washington. (LOC)

# FURTHER READING

Bill, Alfred Hoyt, *The Campaign of Princeton, 1776–1777*, Princeton University Press: Princeton, New Jersey, 1948

Flexner, James T., *George Washington, the forge of experience, 1732–1775*, Little, Brown: New York, 1965

——, *George Washington in the American Revolution, 1775–1783*, Little, Brown: New York, 1968

——, *George Washington and the new nation, 1783–1793*, Little, Brown: New York, 1970

——, *George Washington, anguish and farewell, 1793–1799*, Little, Brown: New York, 1972

Freeman, Douglas S., *George Washington, a biography* (5 vols.), Scribner: New York, 1948–57

Frothingham, Richard, *History of the siege of Boston, and of the battles of Lexington, Concord, and Bunker Hill*, Little, Brown: New York, 1873

Gallagher, John J., *The Battle of Brooklyn, 1776*, Castle Books: New York, 2002

Rice, Howard C. (translator, editor), *The American campaigns of Rochambeau's army, 1780, 1781, 1782, 1783*, Princeton University Press: Princeton, NJ, 1972

Washington, George, *The George Washington Papers at the Library of Congress*, Library of Congress: Washington, DC, available online at:
http://memory.loc.gov/ammem/gwhtml/gwhome.html

# INDEX